SHIPS, SHAWLS
AND
LOYAL SERVICE

THE STORIES OF THREE EAST ANGLIAN BROTHERS

DAVID BLAKELY

Matador
9 Priory Business Park,
Wistow Road, Kibworth Beauchamp,
Leicestershire. LE8 0RX
Tel: 0116 279 2299
Email: books@troubador.co.uk
Web: www.troubador.co.uk/matador
Twitter: @matadorbooks

ISBN 978 1785893 308

British Library Cataloguing in Publication Data.
A catalogue record for this book is available from the British Library.

Printed and bound by CPI Group (UK) Ltd, Croydon, CR0 4YY
Typeset in 11pt Aldine401 BT by Troubador Publishing Ltd, Leicester, UK

Matador is an imprint of Troubador Publishing Ltd

CONTENTS

PLATES

FAMILY TREES

PREFACE

This book has its origin in the extensive family tree drawn up early in the twentieth century by one of my great-uncles, Bernard W. Blakely, but a family tree by itself is of little interest except to those whose ancestors it contains. The main purpose of the book is to tell the stories of three nineteenth-century brothers, each of whom saw some success in his chosen occupation, but in quite different ways from the others in what he achieved. Two introductory chapters tell how these Blakely brothers were descended from the families of Grey and of Rix, who lived in a small Suffolk manor house called Goswold Hall, and how their grandfather, an Ipswich businessman, earned his living.

Bernard Blakely died in 1949 but his handwritten family tree remains in the family's possession. Many of the names on it have dates of birth, marriage and death, and some are accompanied by a few lines of typed notes. His sources of information included parish registers and some manuscripts which were then held at the British Museum; it was a very detailed piece of research for its time. In the twenty-first century there is much more information easily available and I have considerably increased the extent of what Bernard knew about the family. In particular the stories of some of those who lived in the eighteenth and nineteenth centuries are worthy of a wider readership, as their lives influenced many more people than those of their immediate family. Their careers ranged over the provision of stagecoach transport, naval and military actions in Europe and the East Indies, the Nonconformist churches of Norfolk, trade between England and the Far East, and the East Anglian textile business.

The writing of this book would not have been possible without the resources found at the British Library, the National Archives and the Record Offices at Ipswich and Norwich, together with a large amount of material which is now on the internet. I am grateful to the staff at these places and to those who make material available at the click of a mouse. Notes at the end of each chapter are included to supply references and to enlarge on some points without spoiling the flow of the narrative.

I am greatly indebted to Bernard Blakely for having carried out the original research, without which I would perhaps not have started my own investigations. Other family members, past and present, have provided many valuable details. Goswold Hall still stands, and I am grateful to the present owners for inviting me to look round and see the restoration in which they are engaged. I must also thank Mrs Elizabeth Conran for her expertise and advice concerning the Gainsborough portrait. And lastly, a word of thanks to my wife Ruth, a medieval historian, who has pointed me in the right direction on many occasions.

David Blakely
Barnard Castle, Co. Durham

ABBREVIATIONS

BL   British Library

DNB   *Oxford Dictionary of National Biography* (Oxford, 2004)
         online edition at <http://www.oxforddnb.com/>

EIC   East India Company

ERO   Essex Record Office

IOR   India Office Records at the British Library

NRO   Norfolk Record Office

P.P.   Parliamentary Papers

TNA   The National Archives, Kew

SRO   Suffolk Record Office
         (Ipswich branch unless otherwise stated)

The Blakely family arms
Plaque made by J. Frederick Blakely
Photograph © David Blakely

1

THE GREY AND RIX FAMILIES OF GOSWOLD HALL

Thrandeston is a small village in the north of Suffolk near the border with Norfolk. Some of its houses surround the village green which is known as Little Green, while others are further away, including several farms round the Great Green, for the community has always been based on farming. As with many villages the shop, post office and inn are no longer open and villagers have to travel either to Eye, the nearest town in Suffolk, or to Diss in Norfolk. The parish church, an ancient building dedicated to St Margaret of Antioch, is near Little Green and regular services are held there, but it is more than eighty-five years since it was the only parish in the rector's care. Today the parish is in the North Hartismere group and its incumbent has seven churches to look after.

The name Hartismere goes back about a thousand years, for in Domesday Book the Hundred of Hartismere comprised thirty-five places in this area, including Thrandeston which was one of the larger settlements with about fifty households.[1] In the following centuries Thrandeston had five manors: Woodhall, Mavesons and Ampners, all of which belonged at some time to the Cornwallis family, Welholmes and Goswold. It is with the last of these that this book is concerned, for it was owned successively by the families of Grey, Rix and Blakely from about 1473 until 1821.[2]

Although there are several references in Domesday Book to Thrandeston, the manor of Goswold does not appear. However, a certain Walter the Crossbowman is mentioned in the Hundred of Hartismere, and this Walter was the person to whom William the Conqueror granted the manor of Goswold in 1086.[3] Nearly a century later, in 1166, Robertus de Gosewald held a third of a knight's fee of the honor of Eye, and in 1327 Johanne de Gosewolde paid two shillings in the Suffolk Subsidy.[4] In 1462 John Curteys, of Brockford in Wetheringsett, instructed the executors of his will to sell his tenement called Goswaldes.[5] At that time a tenement was land or property held by tenure, rather than its later meaning of a building or an apartment in a large block; in this case it would refer to a parcel of land, probably including a dwelling place. It appears that Goswaldes was bought by Peter Herfrey and he passed it to his son, also called Peter. The family of Herfrey were landowners in the area around Thrandeston and by 1473 the daughter of the younger Peter was married to Richard Grey.[6]

THE GREY FAMILY

Evidence for the pedigree of this family of Grey is found primarily in the records of the College of Arms. For about 150 years from 1530 the Heralds of the College undertook visitations in order to make grants of arms to families in many parts of England, and to record details of those families to whom arms had previously been granted. The records of the College of Arms are not open to public inspection, but copies of many of the arms and pedigrees are found in the extensive set of Harleian manuscripts in the British Library. There are some manuscripts in this collection which record the pedigree of the Greys of Thrandeston for several generations from Richard Grey.[7] One of these shows that Richard was "of Goshold in Suff" and that he was married to the daughter of "Petter Harfrey" in the thirteenth year of King Edward IV, which ran from 4 March 1473 to 3 March 1474. None of the Harleian pedigrees begins earlier than Richard Grey, but in the records of the College of Arms there is a pedigree which shows that Richard was the son of Sir Henry Grey of Ketteringham, who was Sheriff of Norfolk in 1433–4.[8] This pedigree also shows that the arms held by Sir Henry Grey and Richard's grandson Thomas were identical. William Hervey, making his visitation as Clarenceux King of Arms in 1561, must have been convinced that Richard was the son of Henry. The ancestry of Sir Henry Grey is well documented and can be traced back to the Greys of Heton in Northumberland, but the pedigrees state that Henry died without any direct descendants. Although the College of Arms does not now have the evidences necessary to prove that the claimed paternity is correct, it is certain that Richard Grey was the first Grey of Goswold and that his descendants continued to live there for almost 350 years. The Grey family tree is shown in Figure 1.

Ownership of the Goswold estate by the Greys continued from father to son, although not always to the eldest son. The Greys are best described as a family of gentlemen farmers who lived reasonably amicably alongside the owners of the neighbouring properties in Thrandeston and the surrounding villages. Nevertheless, as often happened in the Middle Ages, there were disputes which had to be settled in the courts. One of these involved a watercourse which resulted in an action in the Court of Star Chamber, which Thomas Grey initiated against Sir John Cornwallis in 1542.

The Shermans were another powerful family who caused some problems for the Greys: between 1537 and 1545 there were several court cases between Thomas Sherman and

The Grey and Rix families of Goswold Hall

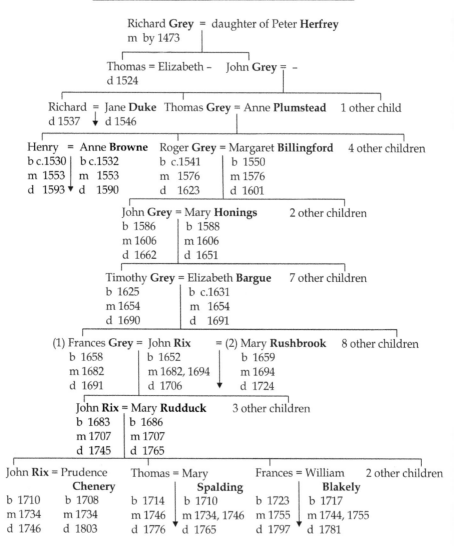

Figure 1

Goswold Hall, Thrandeston
Photograph by Bernard Blakely, c. 1905
Plate 1

Thomas Grey for allowing cattle to stray onto the other's property and for trespassing.[9] One of Thomas Grey's daughters, Sybil, married Thomas Sherman's son Francis in 1557, so perhaps peace was eventually established. Some years later, in 1586, Francis levied a fine of the manor against Roger Grey, who held the Goswold estate at that time.[10] Roger's son John was the next lord of the manor, and in 1640 he was charged 12s 6d for the ship money tax; six other landowners in Thrandeston were charged more than this amount.[11]

The present building of Goswold Hall dates from the late sixteenth century. A fair amount of alteration and extension has been carried out since that time but the oldest parts are at the southern end, shown on the left of Plate 1.[12] It is a farmhouse, set back from the highway from Ipswich to Norwich by a long drive, and surrounded by a moat, which is a common feature of similar houses in this part of East Anglia. In 1674, when Timothy Grey owned the estate, Goswold Hall was assessed for the hearth tax on the basis of the nine hearths it contained. There were two other houses in Thrandeston with as many as nine hearths, but none had more. To give some idea of the relative sizes of houses, mansions had more than twenty hearths, while squires' houses usually had between ten and twenty. So Goswold Hall was not a particularly large house.[13]

Several of the Greys married ladies of some social standing. In 1553 Henry Grey married Anne Browne, whose father Robert was a Baron of the Exchequer, and Henry's brother Roger married Anne Browne's niece Margaret Billingford in 1576. John Grey married Mary Honings in 1606. Mary's mother was descended from the extensive Wingfield family of Letheringham, two members of which had been Sheriffs of Norfolk and Suffolk. The father of Timothy Grey's wife, Elizabeth Bargue, was also a Baron of the Exchequer. Thus the Greys would have regarded themselves, and no doubt have been regarded by others, as gentry: they had a coat of arms but were a little lower in the social scale than the family of Cornwallis.

The Greys' ownership of Goswold Hall ended with Timothy Grey's generation. Timothy had nine children with his wife Elizabeth, of whom five were still alive when he wrote his will in 1689. In his will Timothy left to his wife "all my Estate in Thrandeston and Yaxle[y] for and during her naturall life".[14] There is no specific reference to Goswold Hall, but it would have been part of his lands in Thrandeston and so it passed to Elizabeth when Timothy died in January 1690 at the age of sixty-five. Elizabeth continued to live there, but she died in June of the following year and her daughter Frances died just a few days later. By the terms of Timothy's will all his properties had then to be sold by his executors and the Goswold estate was bought by John Rix, who had been the husband of Frances.

THE RIX FAMILY

John Rix was born in Palgrave, a neighbouring parish to Thrandeston, and he was a husbandman and carpenter.[15] He had married Frances Grey at Thrandeston in 1682 and they lived at Palgrave, where their four children were born between 1683 and 1690. John married his second wife in 1694; she was Mary Rushbrook from Fakenham Magna and they had five children, all of whom were baptised at Thrandeston. Not very much is known of his ancestry but they were a well-to-do family, for he was a gentleman in the days when to be a gentleman was an indication of some status. Evidence for this is found in Thrandeston churchyard where there is a plaque with this inscription:

VAULTS
OF THE FAMILY OF
JOHN RIX, GENTLEMAN, DIED 1706
AND FRANCESCA, HIS WIFE
DAUGHTER OF TIMOTHY GREY, GENTLEMAN,
OWNERS SUCCESSIVELY
OF GOSWOLD HALL

Above the inscription is the Rix coat of arms, but it is not known to whom the original grant of arms was made. This plaque was put up in the nineteenth century when two palisaded tombs were demolished, on one of which was an inscription similar to that above, referring also to William the Conqueror's grant of the manor of Goswold to Walter de Bowyer. Thus the Rix family, whose family tree is shown in Figure 1, became the owners of Goswold Hall and they continued to manage the farm for the next eighty years or so.

Further evidence of the prosperity of the Rixes is found in two examples which largely survive today. The first is the existence of a dovecote situated near the long drive in front of Goswold Hall. This has been dated to early in the eighteenth century, so it would have been erected during the ownership of either John Rix or his son John, who was in occupation from his father's death in 1706 until 1745. Dovecotes were built in order to provide a supply of fresh, tender pigeon meat mainly during the summer and autumn. From the seventeenth century any landowner was entitled to build a dovecote on his own land, the right to do so having previously been granted only to lords of manors and parish priests. The Goswold Hall dovecote was a building of high quality, built by skilled craftsmen.[16] It would have been in use for about a hundred years until the practice of keeping pigeons for food began to decline in the early nineteenth century. Thereafter the condition of the structure began to deteriorate: by the beginning of the twentieth century iron tie-bars had been inserted to prevent the walls from collapsing. It was badly damaged in the storm which lashed many parts of England in 1987, but was saved from complete destruction by emergency scaffolding. In 2009 it was completely rebuilt with grants from Suffolk County Council and DEFRA, and now looks just as it would have done in the days of the Rixes. It is shown in Plate 2.

A major factor which made the reconstruction possible was the existence of a photograph of the building taken early in the twentieth century. This photograph was taken by the Revd Edmund Farrer (1848–1935), an antiquarian who was rector of Hinderclay and Botesdale and who made extensive studies of Suffolk villages, many of which were published in local newspapers. His original material is now at the Suffolk Record Office in Ipswich.[17]

THE RIX FAMILY PORTRAITS

The second example of the Rixes' affluence also has links with Farrer. As he travelled round the Suffolk villages he gathered material for a book detailing the portraits which were to be found hanging on the walls in some of the larger houses, with the intention of publishing his work under the title *Portraits in Suffolk Houses*. In the event it must have proved a much larger task than he expected, for only one part of the work found its way into print: *Portraits in Suffolk Houses (West)*.[18] The other part, *Portraits in Suffolk Houses (East)*, exists in manuscript form and is in four volumes at the Suffolk Record Office in Ipswich. In one of these volumes is an account of six portraits which used to hang in Goswold Hall.[19] By 1923, when Farrer was compiling this section of his work, these portraits had left Goswold Hall more than a century earlier and were in the

Dovecote, Goswold Hall
Photograph © David Blakely
Plate 2

possession of Bernard Blakely in Manchester. The subjects of the portraits are members of the Rix family, and Farrer stated that they were painted by William Hoare in about 1739. He described the portraits in some detail and wrote that five of the sitters were Mr John Rix and his wife, their sons John and Thomas and their daughter Frances. He believed that the sixth, a lady, was possibly Prudence, the wife of the younger John. Bernard Blakely provided the information about the family: as well as being able to quote from oral tradition handed down through the family, he had two letters from his great-aunt Mary Elizabeth Blakely to his father, dated 1871 and 1872. One of these letters gave the names of the first five sitters and said that they were painted by "a Mr Hoare". In the portraits the two sons of Mr and Mrs Rix are shown with indications of their occupations: the younger John Rix was a lawyer in Eye and he is shown holding a book called *The Law of Mortgages*, of which the second edition was published in 1728; Thomas holds an oak leaf, probably because his interest was in managing the farm. Frances is shown as a young girl aged about twelve years.

William Hoare was born in Eye in 1707 or 1708 and spent time in Italy before moving to Bath in about 1739. It would seem that the Rixes knew of this young local painter, who was beginning his career, and they engaged him to paint the portraits. At that stage he was probably glad to have a commission and might not have charged very much, but the fact that the Rixes even considered having a set of portraits painted does indicate that they were a family with aspirations. Later study has dated the portraits about four years earlier than 1739, based partly on the apparent age of Frances; it is also known that Hoare was in London in 1733 and the possible date of 1735 does not conflict with his periods in Italy.[20] When the Blakely family succeeded to the Goswold Hall estate in 1776 they became the owners of the portraits and kept them there until they moved away in 1810. More of the story of the family after this time will be told in the following chapters, but for the moment it will suffice to quote from the second letter of Mary Elizabeth Blakely, who wrote that when the family left Thrandeston,

> the pictures … were tied up in a wrapper for years in a closet I think. They were sent to Norwich afterwards & your Uncle & I had them done up & repaired by Freeman for 9 or 10 pounds.[21]

She also made it clear that ownership passed from eldest son to eldest son and eventually, in 1903, they came into the possession of Bernard Blakely. Bernard was a good amateur photographer and as well as taking photographs of the individual portraits, copies of which are in Farrer's manuscript book and in the family archives, he took two photographs of the six portraits hanging on the walls of his mother's living room in Bournemouth in about 1905.

Bernard and his wife had no children, and when the time came for him to write his will he was of the opinion that none of his nephews had houses big enough in which to hang the portraits. Most regrettably, he decided to split up the set of six and to bequeath them to three museums. Had this happened half a century later his will would have been challenged, but it was not long after the end of the Second World War and his three nephews were busy with their respective jobs. The portraits of Mr and Mrs John Rix were bequeathed to Norwich Castle Museum, not too far from their Thrandeston home; John and Thomas Rix went to the Victoria Art Gallery in Bath, in acknowledgement of the fact that William Hoare spent most of his working life there; young Frances and the "Unknown Lady", as she will now be called, were donated to the Manchester City Art Gallery, perhaps because Bernard lived in Manchester.

Even more regrettable than Bernard's decision to relinquish his ownership of the portraits is the fact that Mr and Mrs John Rix can no longer be seen. For reasons which are not known, Norwich Castle Museum decided to send them to Eye Borough Council in 1956. They were seen in Eye Town Hall by a member of the family in about 1972, but by 1976 they were missing. Their loss was reported in the local press and the police were informed, but no further information has come to light. It is likely that they were either stolen or, probably being unframed, thrown out as rubbish when some office reorganisation took place in Eye town council.

The portraits which went elsewhere have been better looked after. John and Thomas Rix are still in the Victoria Art Gallery in Bath. Both have been properly restored, and they are either on display or else stored and can be viewed by appointment. Frances Rix and the "Unknown Lady" may be seen by arrangement at the Manchester Art Gallery (as it is now called). All four portraits are included in the Public Catalogue Foundation and can be seen on the internet, as they are paintings in public ownership.[22]

The circumstances concerning the "Unknown Lady" make her the most exciting of the six portraits, but there are also some unanswered questions. She arrived in Manchester after Bernard Blakely's death in 1949 and was stored there until 1964 when Elizabeth Johnston, Keeper of Paintings at the gallery, was looking through some of the stock.[23] She realised that, although the painting had been attributed to Hoare, there were some similarities with the early paintings of Thomas Gainsborough in his Ipswich period from 1752 to 1759. Her opinion that the "Unknown Lady" was by Gainsborough was confirmed by John Hayes, the foremost authority on the artist's early work. This attribution earned a paragraph or two in the national press and was described in some detail by John Hayes in his research article "Some

Unknown Early Gainsborough Portraits".[24] The painting is listed in the Manchester Art Gallery catalogue as "Mrs Prudence Rix" but has "Mrs Mary Rix" on the frame. It is shown in Plate 3. An investigation into who she might really be must take account of both the change of artist from Hoare to Gainsborough and also the revised date. For instead of being dated around 1735, if it had been painted by Hoare, the portrait has now been dated about twenty years later, in Gainsborough's Ipswich period. Consideration of the artist will be made in the next chapter, but here it will be explained why neither of the two suggested names for the "Unknown Lady" can be correct.

Prudence was the wife of the lawyer John Rix. John had died in 1746, and by 1755 Prudence was a widow in her late forties. Gainsborough's portraits were known for their lifelike accuracy,[25] and she appears to be rather younger than that age. Furthermore, a widow of any age would be unlikely to have her portrait painted on her own, and Prudence did not remarry. The objection on the grounds of age also applies to Mary, the wife of Thomas Rix, a fact which was mentioned by John Hayes in his article, since Farrer had suggested Mary as a possible alternative to Prudence. There would also be no reason for Thomas's wife to have her portrait painted when that of her husband shows him before his marriage as a young man of twenty-one. In addition, this portrait and that of the young Frances are the same size but smaller than the other four, and a reputable artist would not allow portraits of a husband and wife to be of different sizes.

It seems surprising that Mary Elizabeth Blakely did not mention the existence of the portrait of the "Unknown Lady" in her letters of 1871 and 1872, but it is possible that it was already in the possession of the nephew to whom she was writing. Bernard Blakely provided photographic evidence that all six portraits were hanging together at the beginning of the

"Mrs Prudence Rix"
Painted by Thomas Gainsborough
Image © Manchester Art Gallery, UK/Bridgeman Images
Plate 3

twentieth century, and there is no reason to suppose that the "Unknown Lady" had been acquired by the family at some time in the nineteenth century. She can be regarded as an enigmatic addition to the group of five Rix portraits by Hoare, and the next chapter will provide some clues concerning her true identity.

CHAPTER ONE NOTES

1. Details are in Open Domesday at <http://opendomesday.org/place/TM1176/thrandeston/> [accessed 23 December 2015].

2. W. A. Copinger, *The Manors of Suffolk* (Manchester, 1909), vol. 3, pp. 318–21.

3. Goswold Hall Manor Charter, SRO, HD 291/3. This document, probably written in the late eighteenth century, states that it is a copy of the charter. It may be taken from the Eye Manor Court Book of 1679 when Timothy Grey quoted the original assignation to Walter de Bowyer in evidence that he was entitled to cut furze. See also Vivien Brown (ed.), *Eye Priory Cartulary and Charters, Part One* and *Part Two* (Suffolk Charters Series, Woodbridge, 1992, 1994), vol. 12, p. 15 and vol. 13, p. 71.

4. Hubert Hall (ed.), *The Red Book of the Exchequer* (RS 99, 1896), vol. 1, p. 411; Thomas Hearne (ed.), *Black Book of the Exchequer* (London, 1771), p. 302. Sydenham H.A. Hervey (ed.), *Suffolk in 1327, being a Subsidy Return*, Suffolk Green Books, no. 9, 1906.

5. Peter Northeast (ed.), *Wills of the Archdeaconry of Sudbury, Part I, 1439–1461* (Woodbridge, 2001), no. 1417.

6. Copinger, op. cit., p. 320.

7. BL, Harl. MSS 891, f. 18b; 1136, f. 44; 1169, ff. 116–7; 1449, f. 81; 1560, ff. 180–2. Richard Grey's father-in-law is named in MS 1449.

8. College of Arms, Burke XVIII, ff. 48–9. There is an extensive account of the Greys of Ketteringham in Joseph Hunter, *The History and Topography of Ketteringham* (Norwich, 1851).

9. TNA, STAC2/16, ff. 199–202; Thomas Townsend Sherman,

Sherman Genealogy, including families of Essex, Suffolk and Norfolk (New York, 1920), pp. 35–7.

10. Copinger, op. cit., p. 321; TNA, CP 25/2/220/28/29ELIZIMICH.

11. Vincent B. Redstone (ed.), *The Ship-Money Returns for the County of Suffolk, 1639–40* (Suffolk Institute of Archaeology and Natural History, 1904), pp. 112–3; BL, Harl. MSS 7540–7542.

12. Goswold Hall is a Grade II listed building, reference TM 17 NW, 2/108.

13. Sydenham H.A. Hervey (ed.), *Suffolk in 1674, being the Hearth Tax Returns*, Suffolk Green Books, no. 11, 1905, p. 284.

14. Timothy Grey's will is at SRO (Bury St Edmunds), IC500/2/71/338.

15. Thrandeston burial register for John Rix, 28 November 1706, describes him as "Colonus et Faber Lignarius". SRO, FB124/D2/2.

16. The dovecote is a Grade II listed building. It is described in detail in John McCann, *The Dovecotes of Suffolk* (Suffolk Institute of Archaeology and History, 1998), pp. 60–1 with photographs opposite p. 58 and on the back cover.

17. Edmund Farrer, *Some Old Houses in Suffolk*, in six volumes, at SRO, 728.8094264. The notes on Goswold Hall are in vol. 1, p. 43; the text was published in the *East Anglian Daily Times*, 18 November 1911.

18. *Portraits in Suffolk Houses (West)* was published by Bernard Quaritch (London, 1908).

19. The four volumes are at SRO, q S 92c 22447, 22448, 22449, 22519. The Goswold Hall portraits are described and illustrated in vol. 3, pp. 331–4.

20. Hoare painted the portrait of the freed African slave Ayuba Suleiman Diallo in London in 1733.

21. "Your Uncle" was Edward Blakely (the subject of chapter 5). "Freeman" was William Freeman who was a carver, gilder and picture frame maker in London Street, Norwich.

22. The portraits are at <http://www.bbc.co.uk/arts/yourpaintings>.

The captions are *John Rix*, *Thomas Rix*, *Frances Rix* and *Mrs Prudence Rix* [accessed 23 December 2015].

23. Miss Elizabeth Johnston is now Mrs Elizabeth Conran; she was Curator of the Bowes Museum in Barnard Castle, Co. Durham from 1979 to 2001.

24. John Hayes, 'Some Unknown Early Gainsborough Portraits' in *Burlington Magazine*, vol. 107, no. 743 (February 1965), pp. 62–74.

25. Gainsborough's friends Philip Thicknesse and Elizabeth Orlebar commented on the artist's "good likenesses". Jack Lindsay, *Thomas Gainsborough, His Life and Art* (St Albans, 1981), pp. 78, 116.

2

WILLIAM BLAKELY, COACHMASTER OF IPSWICH

The elder Mr John Rix died in 1745. On his tombstone at Thrandeston he was described as "a townsman highly valuable for his integrity, vigilance and activity. In private life a most loving husband, affectionate father, kind master and friendly neighbour." [1] Goswold Hall passed to his elder son John, but John died in the following year, leaving his brother Thomas to be responsible for the estate. By the time Thomas died in 1776 he had amassed a considerable amount of property and was then living in Eye, although it is clear from his will that he had been living at Goswold Hall. His wife Mary had died eleven years earlier and, having no surviving children, he left all his properties to his sister Frances and her children. In 1755 Frances had married an Ipswich businessman named William Blakely, but in his will Thomas made it very plain that his assets were to go only to those who could claim Rix ancestry: that is, to Frances and her descendants, even if she died without making a will. Perhaps there was some animosity here, but in fact William Blakely was quite wealthy and had property of his own. He is introduced by another passage from Mary Elizabeth Blakely's letter in 1871:

> William Blakely – born Oct[r] 1717 in the City of Rochester in Kent. ... [His children were born] in Ipswich in which Town I think Mr Blakely kept one of

the Inns there, a hotel called the "White Horse" – and
was the first to start a quick coach to London going
I think in two days.

William and his younger brother Lionel were born in
Rochester to parents who were married at Widford, near
Chelmsford in Essex, where there were several families with
the same surname or variations on it. It is possible that their
father, also called William, went to sea, for he was living in
Ipswich when he married Mary Eves and both Ipswich and
Rochester were busy ports in the eighteenth century. Nothing
is known for certain of young William's life until he was in his
mid twenties, but he may have had nautical experience, for
one of his sons and two grandsons were later to spend time
in the Royal Navy or the maritime service of the East India
Company.

THE STAGE-COACH COMPANY

When writing about a grandfather who died eighteen years before
she was born, Mary Elizabeth did not have her facts quite right
about William being "the first to start a quick coach to London",
but she was relaying what had been passed down to her by word
of mouth. Two of the earliest references to coaches travelling the
seventy miles between Ipswich and London in one (long) day
are in 1711 and 1724.[2] The earliest advertisement in the Ipswich
newspapers for a public coach appeared in September 1733 when
Thomas Johnson and John Betts announced that their 'Ipswich
Flying Stage-Coach' would start its winter schedule, taking two
days to London instead of one as in the summer.[3] This was quite
a remarkable speed for that time, but it was only for those who
could afford the fares, which were thirteen shillings for the single
journey and half price for those willing to sit outside.

By 1740 Thomas Johnson had become the senior proprietor with his partner Richard Dave, a coach harness maker who lived at the Coach House in Ipswich, behind the Coach and Horses Inn in Upper Brook Street. The company continued to run coaches to London in one day in the summer, with advertisements being placed in the *Ipswich Journal* in March. In 1743 the announcement was made as usual, but in April Thomas Johnson died and his widow Ann took his place as proprietor with Richard Dave, operating from the Coach House.[4] Late in December they ran a special coach to London which conveyed not only passengers but also parcels, including game, that the people of Ipswich might wish to send to their friends and relatives at the New Year. Unusually, this advertisement stated that there would be six horses to pull the coach: it must have been a heavy load.[5]

Early in 1744 twenty-six-year-old William Blakely was living in Chelmsford and it is likely that he had connections in Ipswich, where his father had come from. In order to travel between these two towns he would have used what had become the 'Ipswich, Saxmundham and Beccles Flying Stage-Coach' and we can speculate that this is how he met Ann Johnson, for in February 1744 he married her and by March he had become the partner of Richard Dave in the stagecoach business.[6] It may be inferred that he had some capital from a previous business, or perhaps from the sale of a naval commission, and was able to buy a share in what was already a prospering company.

For many years it was the only stagecoach company covering the route between Ipswich and London. It advertised that coaches would set out from the Cross Keys Inn in Gracechurch Street in London at three o'clock in the morning, three days a week, to arrive in Ipswich the same night. The return journeys would be made on the following days.[7] The connections to Saxmundham and Beccles ran once a week, and the company also advertised that they could supply a variety of types of coach, "with able horses, at a reasonable rate, to any part of England".

The special journeys for transporting Christmas and New Year goods to London were a regular feature. In 1747 a carriage was advertised to leave Ipswich from Richard Dave's Stage-Coach House early on Christmas Eve, reaching London the same night, and a week later the same journey started from William Blakely's Stage-Coach House. Both houses were in Brook Street, so the families of Dave and Blakely were living close together near to the Coach and Horses Inn. By 1748 the fare for a single journey (inside the coach) from Ipswich to London had been reduced to twelve shillings, with Saxmundham and Beccles to London costing sixteen shillings and eighteen shillings. These prices changed little for many years. A receipt for twelve shillings paid by Robert Barrit for two outside places to London, signed by William Blakely, is in the Suffolk Record Office.[8] The company must have employed a fair number of drivers for their coaches and they made arrangements with inns along the route for changes of horses, which were probably leased rather than being owned.

WILLIAM'S SECOND MARRIAGE

To judge by the regular advertisements there were few changes to the timetable and other arrangements of the Dave and Blakely stagecoach company for the next few years. But early in 1755 there was an event which was to change William's life again, for his wife died and was buried in St Stephen's parish on 9 January. As far as can be ascertained William and Ann had no children, and no evidence has been found of any children from Ann's previous marriage, so William would have been left on his own in the Stage-Coach House. It has been remarked that the circumstances of William meeting Ann Johnson can only be speculated upon. Nor is it known how he met his second wife, for on 1 October 1755 he married Frances Rix of Goswold Hall at Thrandeston church. Their marriage seemed to take place with remarkable speed after the death of Ann and there is no evidence to indicate how they might have met. Although Ipswich was the county town of Suffolk it would not have been a centre for country people from the north of the county. It could be that William was prospecting for a new route for his coaches, perhaps to Norwich.[9] He would have had to pass the entrance to Goswold Hall and perhaps he stopped at the nearby White Hart Inn at Scole – but, again, that is only speculation. Frances moved to Ipswich on her marriage to William, where all their seven children were born over the next ten years.

IPSWICH SOCIETY

One of the well-known residents of Ipswich at this time was Joshua Kirby (1716–1774), a topographical draughtsman who also ran a business painting houses and coaches. Joshua was the son of John Kirby (c.1690–1753), a land surveyor and publisher of *The Suffolk Traveller*, a topographical guide to the county which went into several editions, some posthumously. Joshua also published books including, in 1748, *An Historical Account of the twelve prints of Monasteries, Castles, antient Churches, and Monuments, in the County of Suffolk*. As was the custom at the time, subscriptions were invited before publication, and one of the subscribers was William Blakely. He also subscribed to the second edition of *The Suffolk Traveller* in 1764. It is evident that William was trying to make his way up the social ladder in Ipswich, and he would certainly have engaged Joshua Kirby's business to paint his coaches.

The artist Thomas Gainsborough was another prominent member of Ipswich society. Gainsborough was born in Sudbury in 1727, and while working in Ipswich from 1752 to 1759 he was at an early stage in his career as a painter. Among his friends was Joshua Kirby, who remained close to him throughout his life despite Kirby's move to London in 1755. Having learned his artistic skills in London from 1740 to 1748, Gainsborough continued to visit the city from time to time in order to keep in touch with what was going on in the art world.[10] But his main concern was how to earn enough for his family to live on. Although his "principal love was always for landscape, … demand was limited, and [he] depended upon portraiture for his living. His clientèle was largely among the local gentry." [11] In this he was helped by Joshua Kirby, who had made many contacts through his publication of the *Historical Account* and was able to direct some of his subscribers to Gainsborough. Not only did these commissions produce some much-needed income but they gave him practice in improving his techniques, with the result that his portraits were considered to be very good likenesses.[12]

THE GAINSBOROUGH PORTRAIT

Further consideration can now be given to the portrait of the "Unknown Lady" by Thomas Gainsborough. It is the author's belief that this is a portrait of Frances Blakely, née Rix, painted at the time of her marriage to William Blakely. The evidence for this is circumstantial, but is nevertheless strong.

In the mid 1750s Gainsborough was charging eight guineas for painting a head and fifteen guineas for a half-length portrait, but he was often in debt.[13] In a letter which he wrote to Charles Harris in 1756 concerning a long-standing debt, the artist offered to paint a portrait for Mr Harris instead of paying him the money he owed, as he had done for someone else.[14] When Gainsborough visited London from Ipswich he would have travelled by stagecoach, not being able to afford his own horse or private carriage, and the only company running coaches to London was operated by William Blakely with Richard Dave. The artist's financial problems meant that he might have had difficulty in finding the fare, and instead of paying he may well have offered to paint a portrait of William's new wife.

Furthermore, two portraits which Gainsborough painted during his Ipswich period were of the rector of the parish of Buxhall and his wife, the Revd Henry and Mrs Susan Hill. The Revd Henry Hill's portrait is lost, but that of his wife is now owned by the National Trust and is at Montacute House in Somerset.[15] The relationship between *Mrs Henry Hill* and the "Unknown Lady" is striking, for they are wearing the same lace fichu and pale blue dress; some of the other parts of their attire are also the same, including the yellow bows and pearls. The two paintings are also the same size. It could be that the artist was working on *Mrs Henry Hill* when he offered to paint William Blakely's wife, and he would have saved both Frances and himself some time by using the same clothes and other adornments. It is well known that Gainsborough did not employ other people to paint the backgrounds and other details while he painted the faces of his sitters, but he did use some of the same bows, pearls and so on in several pictures.[16] It was these accessories that drew Elizabeth Johnston's attention in 1964 to the fact that the supposed portrait by William Hoare was by Thomas Gainsborough. Susan Hill was six years older than Frances Blakely and both ladies had many children, some of whom did not survive childhood. A careful study of the dates of birth and death of these children makes the late summer of 1755 the earliest and most likely time for both portraits to have been painted: Frances and William were married at the beginning of October in that year. There is no doubt that the "Unknown Lady" was painted by Gainsborough and as *Frances Rix, Mrs William Blakely* she would have been displayed alone until she joined the five Rix portraits by Hoare at Goswold Hall after the death of Frances in 1797.

THE COACH COMPANY PROSPERS

The Dave and Blakely company was now expanding: by 1761 a second coach to London was advertised, running two days a week and called the 'Ipswich Machine'. It still took a whole day but the departure time was 6 a.m., compared with 1 a.m. for the regular stagecoach. The single fares on this coach were seventeen shillings inside and nine shillings outside, and passengers were allowed only twelve pounds of luggage, whereas on the regular service they could have thirty pounds.[17] It was clearly intended for the Ipswich executive who had business to transact in London. In 1764 another new coach was in use, having steel springs and carrying four inside passengers. This was a fast coach, taking eleven hours including "proper time to breakfast and dine on the road". By this time competition was beginning: another company was in operation on the same route with a post coach running between the Great White Horse Inn in Ipswich and the Black Bull Inn in Bishopsgate, London. The proprietors were innkeepers in London, Brentwood, Chelmsford and Ipswich.[18]

An advertisement for the Dave and Blakely company to take New Year presents to London appeared in late December 1772, but not long afterwards Richard Dave retired from the business. By the summer of 1773 William Blakely had a new partner, Thomas Crawley: their company operated coaches from Halesworth to London in addition to Blakely's existing routes from Beccles,

Saxmundham and Ipswich. The Ipswich post coach to London was now operating under a partnership between Thomas Shave and Charles Harris, the innkeeper of the Great White Horse Inn: it ran from that inn to the Saracen's Head in Aldgate. Two years later, in the summer of 1775, it was announced that a co-partnership had been agreed between Blakely, Harris, Shave and Crawley, and they would operate the post coaches and Ipswich Machine as before. It is clear from the fact that the company was called Blakely & Co. that William had bought out the rival firm. At the same time the new company advertised for a man with experience of bookkeeping and horses, whose wife would be able to undertake the board and lodging of a number of servants: it was evidently a thriving business.[19]

Mary Elizabeth Blakely's belief that her grandfather was the innkeeper of the Great White Horse Inn was not correct, but when the firm of Blakely & Co. was set up its post coaches left from that inn while the company's other coaches departed from the Coach and Horses Inn as before, only about 150 yards away. Furthermore, the company's counting house was at the Great White Horse, so William Blakely did have connections with that inn.[20] Such is the way with oral traditions: facts which are well known to one generation may become rather less certain or embellished in the next generation.

FAMILY MATTERS

William Blakely invested some of his profits from running the stagecoach company in property. In 1762 he bought twenty-five acres of land at Palgrave from the well-known antiquary "Honest Tom" Martin for the sum of £528. It was at that time that Martin had to satisfy his creditors' demands by disposing of some of his book and coin collections, and the sale of part of his property would have further increased his available assets.[21]

It may be speculated as to whether William knew Tom Martin through their mutual interest in fine books or whether the connection was through his wife Frances: Palgrave was not far from Thrandeston and was home to some of the Rix family. In the following year William advertised that he had a family house to let at Wherstead, a village two miles from Ipswich, and in 1773 he put up for sale nineteen acres of pasture and meadowland in Ipswich.[22]

While William was occupied with his business, Frances was at home in Ipswich looking after their growing family. They had three boys and four girls, born between 1756 and 1765, but two of the girls died before their first birthdays and another when she was twenty-one. As has already been mentioned, Frances's elder brother Thomas died in 1776 and she inherited the Goswold Hall estate. Thomas also bequeathed to her his house and land in Eye and it was to that town, rather than to Thrandeston, that Frances moved with her family, either at the beginning of 1777 or perhaps in the following year or two. William may have remained in Ipswich for a time, for he did not retire until March 1780, and it was in Eye just a year later that he died at the age of sixty-three. It was recorded in the *Ipswich Journal* on 24 March 1781 that he had been "for many years a proprietor of the London coaches in this town, but had lately retired from business".

In the late 1770s William's sons were of an age to decide what trade or profession they would follow. The eldest, named William Rix after his father and his mother's family, became the manager of the farm at Goswold Hall. Sadly he did not have long to live, having suffered from a protracted and severe illness, and he died in December 1781. The second son, Thomas, inherited his uncle Thomas's lands at Stradbroke and became a farmer. He was twice married but had no children, and lived until he was eighty years old. The family tree of Frances and William is shown in Figure 2.

The family of Frances and William Blakely

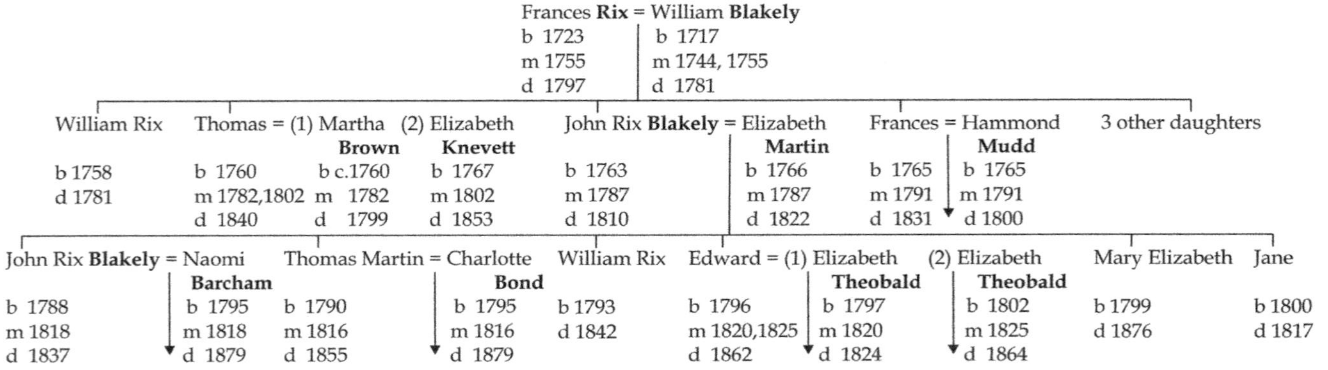

Frances **Rix** = William **Blakely**
b 1723   b 1717
m 1755   m 1744, 1755
d 1797   d 1781

Thomas = (1) Martha (2) Elizabeth   John Rix **Blakely** = Elizabeth   Frances = Hammond   3 other daughters
       Brown   **Knevett**   **Martin**   **Mudd**

b 1760   b c.1760   b 1767   b 1763   b 1766   b 1765   b 1765
m 1782,1802   m 1782   m 1802   m 1787   m 1787   m 1791   m 1791
d 1840   d 1799   d 1853   d 1810   d 1822   d 1831   d 1800

William Rix   Thomas Martin = Charlotte   William Rix   Edward = (1) Elizabeth (2) Elizabeth   Mary Elizabeth   Jane
                     Bond   **Theobald**   **Theobald**

b 1758   b 1790   b 1795   b 1793   b 1796   b 1797   b 1802   b 1799   b 1800
d 1781   m 1816   m 1816   d 1842   m 1820,1825   m 1820   m 1825   d 1876   d 1817
        d 1855   d 1879   d 1862   d 1824   d 1864

John Rix **Blakely** = Naomi
               Barcham

b 1788   b 1795
m 1818   m 1818
d 1837   d 1879

Figure 2

30

JOHN RIX BLAKELY I

The fortunes of the third son, John Rix Blakely, will be followed in more detail, because it is with three of John's sons that this book is particularly concerned. He was born in Ipswich in October 1763. When he was fifteen his name appeared in the subscription list of a new book, *The Naval History of Great Britain*, published in five volumes in 1779.[23] More than 400 people were listed as subscribers, and the publisher noted that these represented about a third of the total. Many of the names were those of naval captains and lieutenants, and the only other person who was stated to be from Ipswich was Thomas Fulcher, a prominent architect. It can hardly be imagined that John's pocket money would have enabled him to buy a subscription, and it may be inferred that his father bought it for him. No doubt he, or his father, had already decided that he would make his career in the Royal Navy. Before John left home his parents arranged for a miniature portrait to be made of him: it is still in the possession of the family and is shown in Plate 4.

At that time one of the routes into naval service for aspiring officers was by securing the patronage of a captain, who could take a specified number of young men as midshipmen. An acquaintance of John's father in Ipswich was Benjamin Page, a tailor and ship-owner and friend of Admiral Sir Edward Hughes, who lived in the town.[24] Mr Page arranged with Sir Edward for his son, also called Benjamin, to join the admiral's flagship as a midshipman and he invited three other boys, John Rix Blakely, Charles Crawley and John Legget Cooke, to join him.[25] Thus in the autumn of 1778 John Blakely started his naval career aboard HMS *Superb*, a third-rate ship of 1,612 tons and seventy-four guns.[26]

On 7 March 1779 the ship left Portsmouth at the head of a squadron which sailed for the East Indies, arriving at Madras in

John Rix Blakely (1763-1810)
Photograph © David Blakely
Plate 4

January 1780. It was not unusual for officers and men to move from one ship to another, and in that year John saw service on board the *Exeter* and the *Sartine* before returning to the *Superb*. In December the ships were occupied in destroying armed ships belonging to the ruler of Mysore, who was attacking territory of the East India Company.

The year 1781 was relatively quiet, but in February and April 1782 Admiral Hughes's squadron was engaged off the south-east coast of India in two fierce battles against the French, for France had allied herself with the United States during the American War of Independence. The French commander was Pierre-André de Suffren but neither side gained a decisive victory: in both actions many officers and men were killed or wounded and much damage was caused to the ships. In the second action, the Battle of Providien, the loss sustained by the *Superb* was particularly heavy, with fifty-nine men killed including the master and two lieutenants. Benjamin Page was among those who were wounded, being badly burnt.[27]

By this time John had learnt many of the skills required by an officer and, with Charles Crawley and four others, he was tested on his knowledge by three of the captains. The admiral gave him a post as acting lieutenant of the frigate *Seahorse* for a month before he was appointed, on 3 June, to be third lieutenant of HMS *Isis*, a fourth-rate ship of fifty guns.[28] He soon saw further action, for the *Isis* was involved in two more sea battles in 1782, neither of which resulted in a clear victory for either side, and more men were killed and ships damaged. Among those who were killed in the Battle of Trincomalee in September was the captain of the *Isis*, the Hon. Thomas Lumley. In April 1783 John was promoted to second lieutenant of the *Isis*; in June the ship was badly damaged in her hull below the waterline in the Battle of Cuddalore.[29] News of the forthcoming peace treaty between Britain and France had not yet reached India, and this was one of the last actions in eastern waters. Admiral Hughes's squadron remained in the East Indies for some time and his flagship became HMS *Sultan* following the loss of the *Superb*, which foundered in November 1783 in a storm in Tellicherry Roads on the Malabar Coast of south-west India. Almost all the crew managed to leave the ship safely.[30]

The other midshipmen from Ipswich were also promoted to be lieutenants on various ships of the squadron but, although the admiral gave them their commissions, these had to be ratified by the Admiralty in London. The only one of the four to have his rank confirmed was Benjamin Page, who eventually became an admiral: his official appointment as lieutenant of the *Eurydice* was dated 20 November 1784 and that ship accompanied the *Sultan*, with Admiral Hughes on board, back to England. The two ships arrived at Portsmouth in May 1785.

Earlier, in January 1784, the admiral had ordered five ships, the *Monmouth*, the *Isis*, the *Crocodile*, the *Chaser* and the *Combustion*, to sail back to England under the command of Captain James Alms of the *Monmouth*. The *Crocodile*, which had been launched only three years before, sailed fast and brought the dispatches from Bombay. She was wrecked in thick fog off Start Point in Devon in May, but all her crew were saved. John Blakely remained on board the *Isis* and his ship and the *Monmouth* reached Spithead, the anchorage between Portsmouth and the Isle of Wight, in June. Charles Crawley had been appointed lieutenant of the *Chaser*, which arrived at Portsmouth with the *Combustion* in mid July. The *Isis* was finally paid off at Chatham at the end of July.[31]

John would have received occasional letters during the time that he was at sea, and so he would have known that his father and elder brother William had died in 1781. After William's death it appears that Goswold Hall was let to tenants for a time, as all the farming equipment and stock were sold by auction in February 1782. When John reached home in the summer of 1784 he decided that his naval career should come to an end, and he turned his attention instead to managing the farm at Goswold Hall. Three years later he married, on her twenty-first birthday, Elizabeth, daughter of Matthew and Sarah Martin who lived at Newton by Castle Acre, some twelve miles to the east of King's Lynn. If it seems rather far from Thrandeston for the two young people to have met, it can perhaps be explained by an advertisement which had appeared in the *Ipswich Journal* in March 1740, offering a reward for information regarding two horses stolen from William Martin's stables in Newton by Castle Acre: claimants were to contact either Mr Martin or Mr John Rix of Thrandeston. These two men were the grandfathers of Elizabeth Martin and John Rix Blakely, and it is evident that the Martin and Rix families had been acquainted for well over forty years.

John and Elizabeth settled in at Goswold Hall and were soon bringing up a young family, for their six children were born at Thrandeston between 1788 and 1800. The following chapters relate the stories of the lives of John Rix, William Rix and Edward. The other children, Thomas Martin, Mary Elizabeth and Jane, are mentioned in passing.

The majority of the population of the area round Thrandeston were involved in one way or another with agriculture and John would have known many of the other farmers and landowners very well. In 1795 his name appeared among forty-two objectors in the Hundred of Hartismere to a proposed tax on market carts, on the grounds that it was "highly oppressive to the trade and agriculture of this kingdom". The announcement in the local press also expressed their willingness to join with other groups in Suffolk to apply to Parliament for a "redress of this grievance".[32] They were supported by the Member of Parliament for Suffolk, Sir Charles Bunbury, who sought relief of the tax, which was the same as that for chaises. But it was not until 1798, after an exchange in the House of Commons with the Prime Minister William Pitt, that he managed to secure exemption for owners of carts from this tax.[33]

In December 1797 John's mother, Frances, died. She had moved back to Thrandeston from Eye after the death of

William and died at the cottage next to Malt House Farm, which had been owned by her family for many years. Her furniture and equipment for brewing were sold by auction at the beginning of January, the sale taking two days.[34] John and Elizabeth's eldest child was then nine years old: the story of his life, with its many different aspects, is recounted in the next chapter.

CHAPTER TWO NOTES

1. The table tomb on which this inscription was written is no longer in existence. The transcription is taken from Davy's *Suffolk Collections*, vol. XIV, BL, Add. MS 19090, f. 197b; this folio comprises 'Further notes communicated by Mr Darby'.

2. For 1711 see 'Diary of a journey from London, by Ipswich and Harwich, to Holland … by James Thornhill', BL, Add. MS 34788, f. 3: his party of five left the Cross Keys Inn in London at 3 a.m. and arrived at Ipswich about 10 p.m. the same day. For 1724 see Daniel Defoe, *A Tour Thro' the whole Island of Great Britain* (London, 1724), p. 67, but he states only that the coach took one day.

3. *Ipswich Gazette*, 1 September 1733.

4. Thomas Johnson's burial on 16 April 1743 was recorded in the burial register of St Stephen's, Ipswich. SRO, FB107/D1/3. Ann Johnson's role as joint proprietor was announced in the *Ipswich Journal* on 6 August 1743.

5. *Ipswich Journal*, 24 December 1743.

6. William Blakely, a bachelor of Chelmsford, married Ann Johnson, a widow of St Stephen's, Ipswich on 20 February 1744 at St Mary's, Chelmsford. ERO, D/P 94/1/10.

7. *Ipswich Journal*, 3 March 1744. This was to announce the start of the summer timetable on 12 March. This newspaper is the source of most of the information about William Blakely's stagecoach business.

8. The receipt is dated 26 June 1759. SRO, FC124/A3/150/8.

9. Apart from a short-lived attempt in 1739–41, the coaches from Norwich to London did not take the route through Essex. Dorian Gerhold, *Carriers and Coachmasters* (Chichester, 2005), p. 155.

10. Lindsay, *Thomas Gainsborough*, p. 37; Hayes, 'Some Unknown Early Gainsborough Portraits', p. 69.

11. John Hayes (ed.), *The Letters of Thomas Gainsborough* (Yale, 2001), pp. 8–9.

12. Hugh Belsey, *Thomas Gainsborough: A Country Life* (London, 2002), p. 65.

13. John Hayes, 'Gainsborough's Suffolk Patrons' in *The Painter's Eye:* Catalogue of an Exhibition to Commemorate the 250th Anniversary of the Birth of Thomas Gainsborough (Sudbury, 1977).

14. Gainsborough's letter to Mr [Charles] Harris, 7 May 1756, in Hayes, *Letters,* pp. 5–7. Charles Harris was a wig-maker and innkeeper of the Angel Inn in Ipswich: *Ipswich Journal,* 15 June 1751. Later he was at the Great White Horse Inn and was a business partner of William Blakely. The other creditor mentioned was Lambe Barry (1704–68), who was High Sheriff of Suffolk in 1748; he had married Susan Morse at Thrandeston in 1738. His portrait is in Ellis Waterhouse, *Gainsborough* (London, 1966), Plate 32 and p. 53.

15. The caption of the portrait is *Susan Murrill (1717–1794), Mrs Henry Hill*; it can be seen on the internet at <http://www.bbc.co.uk/arts/yourpaintings> [accessed 2 January 2016]. See also Waterhouse, *Gainsborough*, Plate 31 and p. 74.

16. "As for millinery, it was not for nothing that Gainsborough had sisters in that trade. He had their eye for fine fabrics, not just a 'face-painter' as many were, employing someone else to do the clothes." John Bensusan-Butt, *Thomas Gainsborough in his twenties* (privately printed, Colchester, 1993); there is a copy at SRO (Bury St Edmunds).

17. Advertisement in *Ipswich Journal*, 4 April 1761.

18. Both companies had advertisements in the *Ipswich Journal* for several weeks from 8 September 1764.

19. *Ipswich Journal*, 3 June 1775.

20. In 1779 the counting house of the company at the Great White Horse was broken into, but the thief was disturbed and nothing was taken. *Ipswich Journal*, 13 February 1779.

21. Details of the purchase are in 'Papers of Taylor family of Diss', NRO, MC 257/23/4; David Stoker, 'Martin, Thomas (1697–1771)' in *DNB* [accessed 23 December 2015].

22. *Ipswich Journal*, 20 August 1763 and 20 November 1773.

23. Frederic Hervey, *The Naval History of Great Britain; from the earliest times to the rising of the Parliament in 1779* (London, 1779). The subscription list is in volume I.

24. J.K. Laughton, 'Hughes, Sir Edward (*c.*1720–1794)', rev. Roger Knight, in *DNB* [accessed 23 December 2015].

25. Benjamin Page gave the names of his three companions, who all became lieutenants, in his journal: 'Extract from the Journal of Admiral Benjamin William Page', in Sir John Knox Laughton (ed.), *The Naval Miscellany* (Navy Records Society, 1912), vol. II, p. 413. Details of Page's naval career are in David L. Jones, 'Admiral Benjamin William Page, 1765–1845' in *The Suffolk Review*, vol. 4, no. 6 (Summer 1979), pp. 269–79; J.K. Laughton, 'Page, Benjamin William (1765–1845)', rev. Andrew Lambert, in *DNB* [accessed 23 December 2015].

26. John Rix Blakely's service in the Royal Navy can be found at TNA in the pay-books and muster rolls for the ships named in the text; his surname is sometimes spelt Blakeley. In most cases the ship from which he came and the ship to which he went are given.

27. Jones, 'Admiral Benjamin William Page, 1765–1845', op. cit., p. 273; Joseph Allen, *Battles of the British Navy* (London, 1852), vol. 1, p. 329.

28. *Official Journal of Rear-Admiral Sir Edward Hughes (?1720–94) as Commander-in-chief of His Majesty's Squadron in the East Indies*, BL, MSS Eur F27–29. This journal, in three sections, is the admiral's day-to-day account of the activities of the squadron from 1778 to 1785. It includes his reports on the sea battles and the promotions of officers throughout the ships under his command.

29. Lists of the ships and casualties in all five actions are in Robert Beatson, *Naval and Military Memoirs of Great Britain from 1727 to*

1783 (London, 1804), vol. VI, pp. 297–9, 354–60. Accounts of the four battles in 1782 are in Hon. Sir Edward Cust, *Annals of the Wars of the Eighteenth Century* (London, 1862), vol. III, pp. 304–20. The Battle of Cuddalore in 1783 is described in Isaac Schomberg, *Naval Chronology; or, An Historical Summary of Naval & Maritime Events ... to the Treaty of Peace, 1802* (London, 1802), vol. II, pp. 143–4. The admiral's letters to the Admiralty in London, reporting on the actions in which he was engaged, are in the *London Gazette* for 26 November 1782, 12 April 1783 and 10 January 1784. The damage to the *Isis* in 1783 is recorded in Admiral Hughes's *Official Journal* (op. cit.).
30. Books of Vice-Admiral Sir E. Hughes, TNA, ADM 7/742; Master's Log of the *Superb*, TNA, ADM 52/2531.
31. Captain's Log of the *Isis*, TNA, ADM 51/484. This covers the period during which John Blakely was an officer. For the loss of the *Crocodile*, see *Ipswich Journal*, 15 May 1784. Some of the wreckage is still among the rocks near Start Point.
32. *Ipswich Journal*, 9 May 1795.
33. R.G. Thorne, *The House of Commons, 1790–1820* (London, 1986), vol. 3, pp. 300–1.
34. *Ipswich Journal*, 30 December 1797.

3

JOHN RIX BLAKELY, MINISTER OF WORSTEAD BAPTIST CHURCH

John Rix and Elizabeth Blakely's eldest child was also called John Rix, maintaining the family's link with earlier generations. His life was quite short, even for that time, but he travelled to parts of the continent of Europe and to Ireland before returning home to East Anglia and becoming a much-respected pastor to a rural church congregation in Norfolk.

Much of the information about John's life is obtained from a book entitled *Brief Memoirs of John Rix Blakely*, which was written by the Revd James Puntis in 1838 (with a second edition in 1840).[1] In the preface to the book Puntis records the fact that his information concerning John's life from boyhood to just before his marriage was obtained from a manuscript in John's own handwriting. This, he wrote, had been drawn up "for the gratification of a near and endeared relative", and there was no intention that its contents would reach a wider readership.[2] Indeed, as John was dying he requested that it should be destroyed: fortunately his family decided otherwise. Although the manuscript is no longer in existence its substance has been preserved in Puntis's book and, now, here.

John Rix Blakely II was born at Goswold Hall on 18 December 1788 and baptised at Thrandeston a week later, on Christmas Day. The incumbent at the time was William

Palgrave, who had held the office for more than thirty years. He remained until his death in 1799, having also been rector of Palgrave for most of the time.

JOHN'S TIME AS A MIDSHIPMAN

As a child John suffered occasionally from depression, and appeared to be unfitted for any active service. Nevertheless, he was keen to go to sea. It may also be that his father regretted not having spent as much time in the Royal Navy as he would have liked, and decided that his son should do what he had been unable to do. John's father had maintained his acquaintance with Benjamin Page, with whom he had been a midshipman on HMS *Superb*. Page had remained in the navy, and in December 1796 he was promoted to the rank of captain.[3]

In 1799 he was back in England being treated for a swelling in his right knee. John's father took the opportunity of seeking, and obtaining, a place for his son as a midshipman on Page's ship, for in January 1800 Page was appointed captain of HMS *Inflexible*, a third-rate ship of sixty-four guns. For John Rix Blakely I to have set his son up as a midshipman must have required considerable expense: the kit list for a midshipman in the maritime service of the East India Company is detailed in Hardy's *Register of Ships* and the conditions in the Royal Navy were similar.[4] But Puntis notes that young John's father did have sufficient income, arising from his own time at sea and from his father's estate, to cover the required costs.[5] Thus, towards the end of February 1800, John made his way to Harwich and sailed from there to Chatham to join the *Inflexible*, which was preparing for a voyage to the Mediterranean.[6]

The ship was being fitted out as a troop carrier in preparation for what was later known as the Egyptian Expedition.[7] Towards the end of March two battalions of the 17th Regiment of Foot marched from Dover to Deal, where they embarked on the ship. A total of 5,000 troops boarded the *Inflexible* and fourteen other ships; on 8 April, having been delayed by the weather, the fleet sailed under sealed orders with Captain Page in command. It was 24 April before they left English waters, and on 13 May they reached the first landing place, Port Mahon on the island of Minorca, where the troops disembarked. John Blakely must have impressed his officers, for at this point in the voyage he received a promotion: his official designation on board had been a Boy of the 3rd Class, and he was now promoted to a Boy of the 1st Class. These terms had been in use for six years, in an attempt to regularise the way in which young gentlemen were recruited to the Royal Navy.[8]

The *Inflexible* then sailed to Genoa to deliver stores to Lord Keith's squadron, which was blockading the city. After that they sailed along the coast to Leghorn (Livorno), where they remained for two weeks before they were ordered to return to Genoa, the city having surrendered on 7 June. The Genoese garrison of more than 8,000 French soldiers was to march to Nice, but those who were sick and wounded were to be transported by sea to the neighbouring port of Antibes, for which task the *Inflexible* was one of the ships used. Towards the end of June the ship started on the return voyage to England, calling first at Minorca, then at Gibraltar, from where they sailed in a small convoy to Lisbon. A change of plan there resulted in the *Inflexible* escorting a large convoy of some forty merchant vessels back to England. Winds and currents meant that their course took a wide sweep into the Atlantic Ocean; eventually the convoy reached the Downs, off the coast of Kent, on 5 August. In mid September Captain Page's ship returned to the Mediterranean and was occupied mainly in transport duties for Lord Keith's campaign for about fifteen months. But young John Blakely was not on board, for he had already had enough of the sea.

Midshipmen at that time were usually young, like John, but because they exercised petty authority over the ordinary seamen they were not popular members of the crew. Living conditions were not good, even for junior officers, and the general tenor of life on board was far removed from what John had been used to in rural Suffolk. As a result, away from the gentle influence of his parents, he rapidly descended into the depths of immorality which were in evidence all around him on board. Later on he bitterly regretted the effect which this had upon him, but for several years he lived "without the fear of God before my eyes".[9] On his return to England he obtained permission to visit his parents, but was so depressed that his family thought that his health was unsuited to the rigours of a seafaring life and he did not return to the navy: his discharge was granted by Vice Admiral Graeme, Commander-in-Chief of the Nore, on 15 September.[10] Instead his father sent him to the grammar school at Ipswich, where he stayed for four years. He learned French, Latin and English Literature and made respectable academic progress, but he also made "considerable progress in immorality", building on what he had learned while at sea.

HIS LIFE IN THE ARMY

In 1804, at the age of nearly sixteen, he had to decide what direction his life was to take. He was by this time clearly set on a life where he would be able to join in all kinds of pursuits with others and, being ambitious, he decided to join the army. His father gave him his full support and used his local connections to obtain for him an ensigncy in the Suffolk Militia. Buying an ensigncy was a common, if expensive, way of entering the army. It cost around £400 at this time, possibly with agent's fees in addition, so his father must still have had money available to spend on his children. The ensigncy in the Suffolk Militia was obtained through John Rix Blakely I's acquaintance with the Cornwallis family, whose family seat at Brome Hall was near Thrandeston. Charles Cornwallis, the first Marquess Cornwallis, was a prominent politician who served two terms of office as Governor General of India, and who, in between, was Lord Lieutenant of Ireland from 1797 to 1801. His only son, also named Charles, was a landowner and Member of Parliament for Suffolk from 1796 to 1805: until his father's death in India in October 1805 he was styled Viscount Brome. Although the younger Charles's health was not good and his father had not wanted him to have a military career, he had been a captain in the Suffolk yeomanry and from 1802 was colonel of the Suffolk Militia.[11] During the autumn of 1804, after John had left Ipswich School, his father must have visited Brome Hall to discuss his son's desired career in the army and John obtained his commission as an ensign in the Eastern Regiment of the Suffolk Militia on 25 January 1805.[12] He was aged sixteen years and five weeks.

In order to join the regiment he had to travel by sea, probably from Great Yarmouth or King's Lynn, to Berwick. A division of the regiment was in that town and he took a coach to Dunbar, where he met the colonel. He then travelled to Haddington and Edinburgh, where he spent a few days before going to Aberdeen ("an uncomfortable passage"), again by sea. Here he acquired his red coat, and spent the next twelve months in Scotland. He tells us nothing of his period with this regiment, except that he had a riotous time and was frequently drunk. It is not known what the regiment was doing in Scotland, and as the History of the Suffolk Regiment indicates that it was in India in 1805, it is likely that there were several sections of it, and part of it remained in the British Isles.[13]

In the following year, and for reasons which are not given, John's father purchased another ensigncy for him in the 20th

Regiment of Foot, which was known at that time as the East Devonshire. Details of his career in this regiment appeared in the Army Lists from 1806 to 1811, with some of the changes in his commission also being recorded in the *London Gazette*. In his initial appointment, dated 2 October 1806, he took the place of Richard Rawson, who was promoted to lieutenant.[14]

Having spent a few weeks at home, he travelled to the Isle of Wight, which was the rendezvous for many regiments. His regiment was then in Sicily, and he was ordered to sail for Malta in a ship called the *Mayflower* in a convoy of about 500 ships. While the ship was at anchor in Spithead, between the Isle of Wight and Portsmouth, he had occasion to go on shore, but was anxious to return late at night in case the ship sailed early the next morning. He secured the services of two men in a small boat, who turned out to be drunk, and on their voyage of about three miles in the dark and in rough weather they lost the rudder and had to use an oar instead. Miraculously, it seems, John saw a light, which was indeed on the *Mayflower*, and he managed to get back on board, much to the captain's surprise. They sailed from England on 4 January 1807 for Gibraltar, where he spent a short time before going on to Malta. The voyage was quite hazardous on account of the weather, but they reached Malta safely on 4 February. A short time was spent there before he sailed in another ship bound for Messina on the island of Sicily. After two days he went with two officers of the Scotch Fusiliers to Melazzo, about twenty miles away, where at last he joined his regiment.

The 20th Regiment had played a leading role in the defeat of a Napoleonic army in the previous year at Maida in southern Italy, in honour of which they were granted permission to add the word "Maida" to their colours, but there was no fighting during the time that John was in Sicily.[15] During the summer of 1807 many of the officers and men were ill with fever and John was among those afflicted, the fever being made worse by the sirocco wind which blew oppressively from North Africa. His illness was also due in part to his intemperate way of life and lack of the comforts he had been used to at home. Nevertheless he found some friends among his fellow soldiers, and one in particular was very kind to him.

Before he had completely recovered from his illness the regiment received orders to return to England and they sailed from Messina on 28 October. At the same time John was promoted to lieutenant, taking the place of H.B. Wood who retired from the army.[16] The transport fleet arrived off Portsmouth on 31 December but quarantine regulations prevented their disembarkation until 7 January 1808.[17] From Portsmouth the regiment marched to Brabourne Lees in Kent, between present-day Ashford and Hythe. Here John's health again declined and he obtained three months' leave of absence, which he spent at home, severely depressed. Eventually he recovered and rejoined the regiment, which was then at Colchester. On 23 June they marched to Ipswich, from where they were to embark for Portugal, but as John's health was still poor he was left in England at the end of July with a section of the regiment that soon moved back to Colchester. Living conditions were not good but he was able to make time for some serious reading of books on travel, history and politics.

After being involved in campaigns in Portugal and Spain, the main part of the regiment returned to England in January 1809, with most of the officers and men being in a very poor state of health.[18] John was reunited with the rest of his regiment and in July they were ordered to march to Dover to embark for Holland. Having spent a week in Dover Castle they marched to Deal, where they embarked on HMS *Agincourt*, a ship of sixty-four guns.[19] The regiment was 950 strong, but the total number of troops who left England at the end of July was nearly 40,000, sailing in about thirty-five warships and a large number of transport ships. This was the disastrous Walcheren Expedition commanded by the Earl of Chatham, which was intended to destroy the French fleet in the Scheldt and to capture Antwerp and Flushing. The 20th Regiment formed part of the reserve and was ordered to sail under the command of Lieutenant General Sir John Hope. They reached Holland in twenty-four hours, landing near Ter Goes on South Beveland Island on 1 August, but they had no provisions or shelter and had to seek food from the nearby farms.

Nor had they any idea of what the rest of the army was doing. Flushing fell on 15 August but Chatham soon abandoned the planned capture of Antwerp, which was well fortified. He withdrew early in September, taking some of the troops back to England, but leaving 15,000 on Walcheren Island where many succumbed to "Walcheren Fever", a form of malaria. The 20th Regiment did not take part in any fighting, although they were on a state of alert for much of the time. John recorded that the reason for the withdrawal was the very poor state of health of the troops and that in his company "there were not more than ten men capable of carrying arms".[20] Such was the condition of the men on their return to England that the regiment needed two years' home service to recover after this expedition.[21] Surprisingly, however, John's own state of health was excellent and, having returned to England aboard the troopship *Bucephalus* on 16 September, he went home on leave until early in January 1810.

During the whole of his time in the army, as earlier in the navy, John had been influenced by the lack of any sense of morality all around him and he was much given to drinking and swearing. When he rejoined his regiment in 1810 he was very ill for a few days, probably on account of being drunk. He resolved to reform himself and, to assist in his task, began reading books of a moral and religious nature. He also bought a prayer book and began to attend church and to read the Bible seriously.

In June, when he was at Colchester, he received a letter to tell him that his father was very ill, and he immediately obtained leave of absence. He arrived at Goswold Hall by the mail coach the next morning, Saturday 9 June, but his father had died a few hours earlier. His father's unexpected death from a stroke at the age of forty-six had a profound effect on John, and when he had to return to Colchester he asked for a further period of leave. The regiment was under orders to go to Ireland and the commanding officer refused the request, but John went straight to the commander of the garrison, General Moncrieffe, and said that if he was not granted leave he would resign from the army. Most generously, the general gave him the leave he asked for, and he returned home for a few weeks.

Although his health was still poor, he left England to join the regiment at Kinsale in southern Ireland at the end of July, but after a few weeks he became so ill that he thought he would die. However, he found private lodgings and in a week had recovered sufficiently to enable him to rejoin the regiment, which by this time had marched the forty miles to Mallow. He was encouraged at this time by visitors, including the clergyman from Kinsale and the wife of the governor of the regiment. He also met with a fellow officer who had been on leave at his home in Cork, still suffering from the illness contracted during the Walcheren Expedition. This officer had come under the influence of an evangelical clergyman at Cork, and John and a third officer accompanied him to the Methodist chapel on several occasions.

In October, when he was once again confined to his room by illness, he had a strong religious experience, which was the turning point of his life. Although he continued to suffer from attacks of depression, his fellow officers and the men under him were well aware that his life had changed. Although some admired him for it, many began to oppress him on account of his new-found religion. As a result of his association with the Methodist church in Mallow and of his own love of reading, he began to organise the men into buying religious books. But some of his fellow officers made a complaint to the commanding officer, with the evidence of the name "Lieutenant Blakely" being found in a box of these books. John's defence was that his conduct was not liable to make his men insubordinate, and he drew the major's attention to the character and behaviour of the men in the regiment who were religious. This met with some sympathy from the commanding officer but he nevertheless ordered him to cease his activities, under threat of a court martial.

But the complainants did not give up, and when the new colonel of the regiment, Sir John Stuart, arrived in Ireland they took their case to him. However, having read some of the books, Sir John found them in no way distasteful and regarded the whole matter as a trivial affair. In fact, Colonel Stuart treated Lieutenant Blakely and the other religious men very kindly and, when John was about to leave the army, he expressed his good wishes to him.

John did not remain very long in Ireland, for by the spring of 1811, with his health still poor, he decided that he was unsuited to a military career and obtained leave of absence from the regiment. After a week at a friend's house in Cork he obtained a passage on a cross-Channel vessel to return to England. On board he met with a minister of one of the independent churches and the two of them travelled to London together, where they spent time in attending the annual meetings of various evangelical societies. This was a new experience for John, but he greatly enjoyed the meetings and profited from them.

Following the death of her husband, John's mother

Elizabeth had moved from Goswold Hall to live at Knapton, near North Walsham, with her son Edward and daughters Mary Elizabeth and Jane.[22] The Goswold Hall farming stock and many household goods were sold at auction, and the farm was rented out for the next ten years until it was eventually sold in 1821.[23] The house where Elizabeth and her family lived at Knapton was rented from Elizabeth's brother-in-law, William Seppings, who lived about two miles away at Swafield House.[24] John arrived at Knapton on 17 May 1811 and his retirement from the army was recorded in the *London Gazette* at the beginning of July.[25] He was only twenty-two years of age.

JOHN BECOMES A DISSENTER

John had spent the early years of his life at Thrandeston, where his family had attended the parish church for many generations, but since leaving home at the age of eleven he had neglected all forms of religion. After his return from Ireland and his decision to reform his life he was anxious to associate himself with the Dissenters, as the members of Nonconformist churches were known at that time. Accordingly he visited Norwich, believing that this would be the most likely place to find the type of church he was looking for. On arrival there on a Sunday morning he was directed to the Old Meeting House in Colegate, the oldest Nonconformist church in Norwich and one of the oldest in the country, built in 1693.

The minister who conducted the service was the Revd Joseph Kinghorn, who John naturally assumed to be the minister of the independent church which met there, but when he called on him the following day he found that he was the minister of the Particular Baptist Church of St Mary's, which was using the Old Meeting House while their own church was being rebuilt.[26] John asked Mr Kinghorn for information concerning independent churches in Norfolk and he was directed to the chapel at North Walsham. Accordingly he introduced himself to the minister there, the Revd James Browne, who asked him to write a letter requesting admission to the church. His letter, dated 22 September 1811, was favourably received and he attended his first communion service in the chapel at nearby Bradfield on the first Sunday afternoon in November. The Revd James Browne was minister of the Independent Meeting Houses at both North Walsham and Bradfield, and John was to have a close friendship with him for the rest of his life.[27]

John's new-found enthusiasm for the type of worship found in the dissenting churches caused him to try to change the allegiance of his family, and especially that of his mother to whom he was deeply attached. Elizabeth's father, Matthew Martin, was head of a well-to-do family who were members of the Church of England, and both he and his own father had been churchwardens for many years. Puntis writes that Elizabeth was strongly prejudiced against Dissenters and evangelical forms of religion, but such was the persuasive power of her son that she did, in part, acknowledge that his views on religion supplied something which she lacked. However, she remained a member of the established church and always took communion there. In the spring of 1812 John was again afflicted by illness and spent three months confined to bed. When he had recovered he was still unable to walk as far as he had previously been able to, and so he moved from Knapton to North Walsham in order to be able to continue to attend services at the independent church there.

The *Brief Memoirs* give no indication of any form of trade or employment that John followed after leaving the army, although an account of the church at Worstead states that he was a schoolmaster.[28] He had been a main beneficiary of his father's estate and inherited land known as Le Tofft or Tyes

Estate, which was let out to tenants. The rent supplemented any income he had from teaching and provided him with sufficient money on which to live.[29] His long bouts of illness provided him with time for reading and he was particularly concerned over the question of believers' baptism, a subject which was much debated in Nonconformist churches during the early and middle parts of the nineteenth century.

He attended the funeral of a friend who was a member of the independent church at North Walsham but whose parents were members of Worstead Baptist Church, situated at Meeting House Hill, which is about two miles from the village of Worstead. The funeral was held there and John introduced himself to the newly arrived minister, the Revd Richard Clarke.[30] Finding the Baptist form of worship agreeable, he began occasionally to attend that church on a Sunday. Further conversations with Richard Clarke on the subject of baptism led him to want to learn Greek and so he moved to lodgings in Norwich, where Joseph Kinghorn was able to find him a tutor in that language. Having become reasonably proficient in Greek, he then began to learn Hebrew under the tuition of Mr Kinghorn, who was "one of the outstanding figures of his day in the Baptist denomination".[31] John's wide reading made the study of these languages quite easy, and after about eighteen months he was convinced of his need to be baptised by immersion. Accordingly he was baptised by Mr Kinghorn on 13 April 1814 and became a full member of the Baptist church, worshipping at St Mary's in Norwich.

WORSTEAD BAPTIST CHURCH

Two years later, circumstances arose which meant that he returned to live with his mother. There is no suggestion in the *Brief Memoirs* of what these circumstances might have been, and it was probably at about this time that Elizabeth Blakely moved the few miles from Knapton to North Walsham, living with John, Mary Elizabeth and Jane. Their brother Edward was now almost twenty and would have started work in Norwich before his mother's move. John's formal dismissal from St Mary's, Norwich, to Worstead Baptist Church took place on 31 March 1817.[32] A few weeks later, on 16 May, his sister Jane died, aged sixteen. She was buried in the parish church of St Nicholas in North Walsham where there is a memorial to her, and her name is also recorded on one of the table tombs in Thrandeston churchyard.[33] In her father's generation four of the seven brothers and sisters had died before the age of twenty-four, but Jane was the only one of John Rix Blakely I's children not to reach the age of forty-eight.

One of the long-serving deacons at Worstead Baptist Church was John Barcham, a farmer who lived at Church Farm, Edingthorpe, about three miles from Meeting House Hill. John's wife Elizabeth had been baptised in 1752 at the independent church at Bradfield which John had first attended in 1811. In 1816 John and Elizabeth retired from their farm to live at Poplar Cottage, a large cottage on White Horse Common within sight of the chapel at Meeting House Hill. There was clearly a close relationship between the Blakely and the Barcham families, for on 14 July 1818 John Rix Blakely signed the register at the marriage of the Barchams' youngest son Ezra at the parish church of All Saints, Edingthorpe. Ezra had taken over the family farm when his father retired.[34] Less than three months later, on 4 October, and at the same church, John married the youngest Barcham daughter, Naomi, who was six years younger than himself, having been born on 2 February 1795. At that time marriages could take place only in churches of the Church of England and the rector, the Revd Richard Adams, conducted both of these services.[35] At John's marriage Naomi's eldest brother Jedidiah and her mother signed the register. James Puntis, writing the *Brief Memoirs*, had a high regard for Naomi, both in her own right and as a wise, prudent and cheerful companion for John, who still suffered from depression. A portrait of Naomi in her old age is shown in Plate 5: it is an early type of photograph known as an ambrotype, and was taken by William Boswell of Norwich in about 1865 when she was seventy.[36]

It was probably soon after John's marriage that his mother moved from North Walsham to Norwich, where her son Edward was setting up in business as a draper. She died in Norwich about three years later, on 4 April 1822, and was buried at Thrandeston. In her will she left John £100 "in token of my approbation of his disinterested conduct respecting his claim on his Father's Estate". Goswold Hall had not been specifically mentioned in the will of John Rix Blakely I and it is likely that the estate was entailed, so that his eldest son would inherit it automatically. In fact, John did not claim his inheritance and when the estate was sold in 1821 the legal owners were his mother Elizabeth and her five surviving children, between whom the proceeds of £8,550 were divided.[37]

On their marriage John and Naomi moved to the village of Worstead, where they stayed for the next eight years or so, during which time their four eldest children were born. In about 1826 the family moved to the hamlet of Meeting House Hill, where their other children were born.[38] Their family tree is shown in Figure 3. John was, from the beginning, an active member of the church. He assisted with teaching the children in the Sunday school and began to make visits to some of the neighbouring villages on Sunday evening, to pray with them and to read them sermons from some of the books in his library. This went on for some time, until he began to preach to them using his own ideas rather than simply reading what others had written. The minister and the church members realised

Naomi Blakely, née Barcham (1795-1879)
Photograph by William Boswell, c. 1865
Plate 5

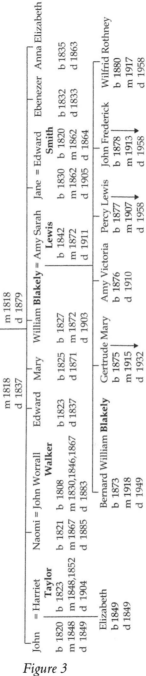

The family of John Rix Blakely

Figure 3

57

that he had ability, despite his natural timidity, and at a church meeting in September 1822 he was formally licensed by the church to continue what he was already doing and to assist the ministers in the neighbouring churches. He also occupied the pulpit of his own church more frequently as the minister, the Revd Richard Clarke, became increasingly incapable on account of his advancing age and illness.

In common with many other dissenting churches, and despite the difficulties of travel in the early nineteenth century, the church at Meeting House Hill drew its congregation from a wide area. Later, in 1836, White's *History, Gazetteer and Directory of Norfolk* stated: "The Rev. J. R. Blakeley, the minister, has a neat residence, with stabling for 25 horses for the accommodation of his hearers, many of whom live at a considerable distance." But the farming folk were accustomed to making long journeys to market and travelling to Meeting House Hill posed few problems. Sundays were full days with two or three long services and picnics in between.

The church had been established in 1717: it owed its foundation to Richard Culley, a farmer who had been unanimously chosen as its first pastor. The original church was a thatched barn beside the brook which was enlarged twice. By the time that John and his growing family were members the church was becoming dilapidated and beyond repair, and in February 1829 it was decided that it should be replaced by a new building to be built on a nearby site. The church records include a list of subscriptions to the New House, one of the largest of which came from the Revd Richard Clarke. He had some private income dating from the time before he became minister and had been pleased to receive much less than the proper remuneration for his work. He made a donation of £10 a year while he remained as minister and left a further £250 in his will. Members of the Barcham family made substantial donations and the "Young Blakelys" gave 12s 6d, a large sum for very young children – perhaps their parents helped. One of Naomi's brothers, Asher Barcham, then of Tonbridge, gave a clock which is still in working order.

The foundation stone was laid on 22 June 1829 and the building was opened for services on 6 October of that year. The Revd James Puntis, author of the *Brief Memoirs*, spoke at the morning service and the Revd Joseph Kinghorn of Norwich addressed the congregation in the afternoon. The Religious Census of 1851 gave the number of seats as 530, with the average attendance at an afternoon service in the summer being 400 and another ninety in the Sunday school. The building still stands and is shown in Plate 6.

In July 1832 Richard Clarke resigned his office as minister through ill health. John received an invitation to fill the post as a probationer for a year, which he accepted. After this time he was unanimously chosen by the church members to be their pastor. He considered himself highly honoured and accepted with "fear and trembling" and many misgivings on account of his own perceived lack of ability for such a responsible position.[39] The date of his ordination was set for 5 November 1833 and the event was reported in the *Baptist Magazine*. A large congregation was present, which included many of the ministers of other Baptist churches in Norfolk. Among those who took part was the Revd John Bane, who delivered the opening discourse on the constitution of a Christian church, asked John the necessary formal questions and received his confession of faith. John Bane had been a sailor who spent eight years in France as a prisoner of war and was baptised by Joseph Kinghorn in 1815; he had been pastor of the church at Aylsham since 1817.[40] The Revd James Puntis spoke the ordination prayer and delivered the charge to the new minister. The Revd James Browne of North Walsham concluded the proceedings with prayer; it will be recalled that John had first met him in 1811. The proceedings made a considerable impression on John, which he remembered with

Worstead Baptist Church
Photograph © David Blakely
Plate 6

special prayers each year on the anniversary.

Only two months later the church members, and John in particular, were saddened by the death of the former pastor. Puntis relates in detail how Richard Clarke had attended a prayer meeting in the chapel on New Year's Day in 1834 and that he died peacefully two days later when John was visiting him. His health had been poor for some time, but he had appeared to be much better in the morning of the day he died. A native of Devon, he was aged sixty-eight and had been pastor for twenty years. His widow Margaret died in February 1844.

John continued his ministry for the next three years, supported by his wife, who knew him better than most. He was still troubled by bouts of depression and a sense of being unsuited for his work, but with the encouragement of Naomi and other members of the church he felt honoured to be their pastor. He took a particular interest in those he baptised who, like himself, had been in the armed services. In the Worstead Church Book, in which the names of those baptised were recorded, he added details of the service history of three such men: these were a marine soldier who had served on HMS *Victory* under Admiral Keppel, a soldier who was in the 16th Dragoons in Spain, and a pensioner from the Foot Guards who had been wounded in the head at the Siege of Valenciennes in 1793.[41]

John and Naomi's second son Edward had, from an early age, expressed a wish to go to sea, following in the footsteps of his father, his grandfather and his uncle William Rix. His parents insisted that he finish his education first, rather than letting him go off for a considerable period of time at a very young age as John had been allowed (or made) to do. They then let the boy go on a voyage as far as Newcastle in the spring of 1837 when he was fourteen. Edward returned home with what appeared to be a very bad cold but it affected his throat and, after three weeks, on 10 June, he died. Most of the family also caught the infection, but none was seriously ill until towards the end of July when John also succumbed to it. It may have been diphtheria, for his throat was badly affected, and although treatment helped, his lack of any reserves of energy caused him gradually to weaken. For the last few weeks of his life he was so weak that he could not move at all nor take any solid food. He suffered greatly for about eighteen weeks, yet Puntis records that his faith strengthened him so that he approached his death in complete peace. He was confident that God would provide for his wife and children and that a successor would be found as minister of the chapel.

He died on Sunday morning, 19 November 1837, at the age of forty-eight, and was buried in the chapel burial ground on the following Friday. His friend the Revd James Browne took the funeral service and the Revd James Puntis preached on the following Sunday. Large crowds of people attended both of these services and, quite unusually for those times, the curate of Worstead parish church, the Revd W. Tylney Spurdens, mentioned him with affectionate respect in a sermon on the subject of death not long afterwards.

John Rix Blakely had been pastor of Worstead Baptist Church for only five years, although he had been a member of the church for much longer. Despite his own feelings of inadequacy his ministry was very well received by the congregation, and he is remembered by a memorial plaque which is still on the wall at the front of the church, underneath the gallery. After his death Naomi went to live not very far away at White Horse Common with her four daughters while her son William was at school in Norwich.

JOHN'S BAPTIST LEGACY

John Rix Blakely was a remarkable man, whose gentle upbringing was followed by several years of complete contrast in the armed forces until his religious experience had the effect of changing his manner of life yet again. He spent the last twenty-six years of his life from 1811 in studying and in preaching to the people of the rural community in north Norfolk. It is sad that his time of office as minister of Worstead Baptist Church was so short, but the fact that he was remembered with affection for many years afterwards is testimony to what he was able to do in the time that he had there.

However, he would have been encouraged to know that his Baptist legacy was to continue in the next two generations. For in 1872 his son William married Amy Sarah, daughter of the Revd Jonathan Preston Lewis, minister of the Baptist Church in Diss; their marriage took place at St Mary's Church in Norwich, where John had worshipped many years before. The ceremony was conducted by the minister, the Revd George Gould, who was distantly related by marriage to Amy's father. Her grandfather, Thomas Lewis, had been brought up in a small hamlet by the River Wye in Monmouthshire, but soon after his marriage he moved to Wales where, in 1809, he was one of the founders of the Baptist Church in Cardiff. Thus the Baptist tradition was firmly rooted in William's family's upbringing. It was William's eldest son, Bernard, who carried out the initial research into the family history. By profession he was an engineer and he was associated for many years with the Baptist College Mission in Manchester, being treasurer and a Sunday school teacher. Another son, Percy, was for much of his life a deacon in the Baptist Church in Ryde, Isle of Wight, in which town he ran a flourishing pharmacy business. And last, but by no means least, William's daughter Gertrude left

England for China on New Year's Day in 1900 as a missionary with the non-denominational China Inland Mission.

At the start of the nineteenth century a young midshipman was travelling in Europe with the British armed forces. He could scarcely have imagined that, a century later, his grandchildren would be engaged in Christian activities which owed their origin to his own involvement in a church in rural Norfolk.

CHAPTER THREE NOTES

1. James Puntis, *Brief Memoirs of John Rix Blakely, late Pastor of the Baptist Church at Worstead, Norfolk* (Norwich, 1838 and 1840). Copies are in the British Library and Norwich Millennium Library (both editions), and at the Norfolk Record Office (1838 edition). There is no difference in the text between the two editions; the later one is smaller in size and contains a note to say how popular the first edition had been. Puntis (1793–1850) was minister of Colegate Street Baptist Chapel in Norwich from 1828.

2. Puntis, *Brief Memoirs* (1838), Preface, p. v. There is no indication of who the relative might have been.

3. Laughton, 'Page, Benjamin William' in *DNB* [accessed 23 December 2015].

4. Charles Hardy, *Register of Ships Employed in the Service of the East India Company from 1760 to 1810* (London, 1811), Appendix, pp. 148–9.

5. Puntis, *Brief Memoirs* (1838), p. 5.

6. *Inflexible* Pay Book 1800-02, TNA, ADM 35/867. John's age is given as 13, although he was only 11 years old.

7. *Inflexible* Captain's Log 1800-01, TNA, ADM 51/1332; 'Historical Memoirs of Admiral Benjamin William Page' in J. Ralfe, *Naval Biography of Great Britain* (London, 1828), vol. IV, p. 258; Æneas Anderson, *A Journal of the Forces which sailed … on a Secret Expedition under the Command of Lieut.-Gen. Pigot, …* (London, 1802).

8. S.A. Cavell, *Midshipmen and Quarterdeck Boys in the British Navy, 1771–1831* (Woodbridge, 2012), p. 88.

9. Puntis, *Brief Memoirs* (1838), p. 7: this part of the book is in John's own words.

10. *Inflexible* Pay Book 1800-02.

11. C.A. Bayly and Katherine Prior, 'Cornwallis, Charles, first Marquess Cornwallis (1738–1805)', in *DNB* [accessed 23 December 2015].

12. *London Gazette* no. 15968, 21–25 October 1806, p. 1393. His surname is spelt Blakeley, as it was throughout his army career.

13. E.A.H. Webb, *History of the 12th (The Suffolk regiment) 1685–1913: Including a brief history of the East and West Suffolk Militia* (London, 1914; 2002 reprint).

14. *Army List* 1806, pp. 150–1 (handwritten additions), TNA, WO 65/56; *London Gazette* no. 15964, 4–7 October 1806, p. 1323.

15. The 20th Regiment of Foot and others were "granted Permission … to bear in their Colours and on their Appointments the Word 'Maida', as an honourable and lasting Testimony of the distinguished Gallantry displayed by those Corps in the Action fought on the 4th of July 1806, on the Plains of Maida in Calabria". *London Gazette* no. 16005, 28 February 1807, p. 258.

16. His appointment was dated 29 October 1807. *Army List* 1807, p. 150 (handwritten addition), TNA, WO 65/57.

17. Major B. Smyth, *A History of the Lancashire Fusiliers, formerly XX Regiment* (Dublin, 1903), vol. 1, pp. 219–21.

18. Smyth, *History of the XX Regiment*, vol. 1, pp. 240–1; Puntis, *Brief Memoirs* (1838), p. 16.

19. John states that he embarked on HMS *Agincourt*. Puntis, *Brief Memoirs* (1838), p. 16. However, an official report on the Expedition states that the 20th Regiment embarked on HMS *Monmouth*, while HMS *Agincourt* carried part of the 4th Regiment. *A Collection of Papers relating to the Expedition to the Scheldt, presented to Parliament In 1810* (London, 1811), pp. 338, 340.

20. Puntis, *Brief Memoirs* (1838), p. 17.

21. J.B. Wilson, 'Dr Archibald Arnott: Surgeon to the 20th Foot and Physician to Napoleon' in *British Medical Journal*, 1975, 3, pp. 293–5.

22. Mary Elizabeth wrote in 1872 that they moved from Goswold Hall in 1810. Thomas Martin, sixteen months younger than John Rix, had probably left home, and William Rix was on his

first voyage as an officer with the East India Company. Edward was fourteen years old in the summer of 1810 and in the autumn of that year was at school in Great Yarmouth.

23. The auction sale was on 3 and 4 October 1810; the sale catalogue is at SRO, HD 291/1. The sale of Goswold Hall was advertised in the *Norfolk Chronicle*, 14 July 1821.

24. William Seppings (1748–1822) was the husband of Elizabeth Blakely's elder sister, Sarah. The Rix family portraits were kept at his house until the family was settled in Norwich.

25. *London Gazette* no. 16500, 29 June–2 July 1811, p. 1204. In the *Army List* 1811, p. 156 (handwritten addition), TNA, WO 65/61, he is stated to have sold his ensigncy on retiring.

26. Joseph Kinghorn had been minister of St Mary's since 1790. His life is fully documented in Martin Hood Wilkin, *Joseph Kinghorn of Norwich, a Memoir* (Norwich, 1855). See also Alexander Gordon, 'Kinghorn, Joseph (1766–1832)', rev. J.H.Y. Briggs, in *DNB* [accessed 23 December 2015].

27. Puntis, *Brief Memoirs* (1838), pp. 45–8.

28. Maurice F. Hewett, 'Early Days at Worstead' in *The Baptist Quarterly*, vol. XL, 1943, p. 173.

29. When John became minister of Worstead Baptist Church he accepted a smaller salary than the congregation would have expected to pay. Puntis, *Brief Memoirs* (1838), p. 106.

30. Richard Clarke was minister of Worstead Baptist Church from 1813 to 1832.

31. C.B. Jewson, *The Baptists in Norfolk* (London, 1957), p. 72.

32. This date is in a note alongside the record of John's baptism at St Mary's Baptist Church, Norwich in the 2nd Church Book: NRO, FC 6, MS 4283, p. 60. Puntis, *Brief Memoirs* (1838), p. 60, states that the dismissal was on 2 June 1816, which he obtained from a list of members in the records of Worstead Baptist Church in the Church Book: NRO, FC 42/1. The Worstead Church Book also shows that, at a church meeting on 23 March 1817, a letter was sent to the church at Norwich "requesting his

dismission from them to us & signifying that on its reciept we should Cordialy recieve him".

33. Jane was born on 7 September 1800. Her baptism is recorded twice in the Thrandeston registers: on 2 October 1800 and on 16 September 1803. It is likely that the first baptism was done privately and the second at a public service, because her brothers Thomas Martin and William Rix were also baptised twice.

34. Christopher J. Farrow and Judith A. Constantine, *The Barchams of Edingthorpe* (privately printed, 2003), pp. 17–23.

35. Richard Adams had been rector since 1789 and remained until his death in 1850. The next incumbent, the Revd Joseph Lawson Sisson, reported that the Glebe House was dilapidated, that the parish had been cruelly neglected for the last 60 years and that the parishioners were, with few exceptions, Dissenters. Janet Ede and Norma Virgoe (eds), *The 1851 Census of Accommodation and Attendance at Worship*, Norfolk Record Society, vol. LXII, 1998; TNA, HO/129/230.64. John Barcham had been Churchwarden of Edingthorpe in the 1780s, probably while also attending Worstead Baptist Church.

36. Ambrotypes were common from the mid 1850s to the mid 1860s. William Boswell junior was the photographer in his father's firm of W. Boswell and Son, who traded as carvers and gilders.

37. Puntis, *Brief Memoirs* (1838), p. 105. The new owner of the estate was Thomas French, a solicitor in Eye.

38. The Family Bible has "Parish of Worstead" against the birth records of the four eldest children, born between 1820 and 1825, and "born on Meeting Hill" against the four youngest, born between 1827 and 1835. A similar distinction is made in the birth registers of Worstead Baptist Church.

39. Puntis, *Brief Memoirs* (1838), p. 71.

40. Jewson, *Baptists in Norfolk*, pp. 60–1. John Bane died in 1850.

41. Worstead Baptist Church, Church Book, NRO, FC 42/2; quoted in Jewson, *Baptists in Norfolk*, p. 60.

4

WILLIAM RIX BLAKELY, CAPTAIN IN THE EAST INDIA COMPANY

William was John and Elizabeth Blakely's third son and was named after his uncle, who had died at the age of only twenty-three. In contrast to his brother John, whose experience of the Royal Navy was short and not at all pleasant, William spent all his working life at sea and, to judge from the position which he finally held, he became a very successful and competent officer in the East India Company's maritime service.

William was born on 14 April 1793 at Goswold Hall. The Thrandeston register records that he was baptised privately on 8 May and then publicly on 1 August. This repetition of the baptism ceremony was not uncommon: both William and his elder brother Thomas were baptised twice, their public baptism being "brought into the church", as it was sometimes described in church registers.

There is no contemporary biography of William, but much of his life at sea can be traced through the records of the East India Company. Later in his life he wrote that he had been sent to sea at the age of twelve: it may be inferred that this would have been as a midshipman in a naval ship similar to that in which his brother spent a short time at about the same age. The fact that both boys started their careers at sea probably arises from their father having done the same but was then frustrated because he had to manage the farm at Goswold Hall instead. It was noted in chapter 2 that William's grandfather may also have had experience at sea before becoming a stagecoach proprietor.

THE EAST INDIA COMPANY

The British East India Company was one of several commercial enterprises formed in Western Europe during the seventeenth and eighteenth centuries to promote trade with the East Indies. The Company was granted its original charter by Queen Elizabeth I on 31 December 1600 and it was a major force in the history of India for more than 200 years. In the early nineteenth century the "Honourable Company" was an immense organisation, with its headquarters at East India House in the City of London. In addition to trading with India and the Far East, particularly China, the Company administered large parts of India until 1858, using its own private armies and personnel.

Ships were needed in order to reach India and other countries in south-east Asia, and the Company operated a large number of vessels. Some of these were owned by the Company, although most were owned by influential individuals on the Company's behalf. In the period from 1800 to the end of trading operations in 1834, about 300 ships were involved at some time in making regular trips to the Far East, mainly to India and China. The largest ships were of about 1,400 tons and all were organised along lines similar to those in the Royal Navy with officers, midshipmen and ordinary seamen, totalling as many as 150 on each ship. The ships sailed in fleets, although the vagaries of wind and weather meant that they were not always in sight of each other. They usually left England in the spring and returned between twelve and eighteen months later, having remained for some weeks or months in India or China in order to unload and load their cargo.

There were three main patterns of voyages: from England to India and back; from England to China and back; from England to India, on to China and back to England. With few landing places on the way they had to be self-sufficient for several months; the amount of fresh water remaining was recorded in the ships' logs every week while at sea. Although the ships were armed they did not often have to use their guns. On the return voyage a landfall was always made at St Helena in the South Atlantic Ocean. The island of St Helena was a colony, governed from the mid seventeenth century by the East India Company on behalf of the British government. During the time of Napoleon's exile on the island, from 1815 to 1821, regular troops of British regiments were garrisoned there.

In the twenty-first century it is taken for granted that documents relating to commercial organisations will be readily available, at least to those who have authority to see them. In earlier times, before the advent of the typewriter and similar methods of keeping records, this was not always the case. But the East India Company was well known for the meticulous manner in which it recorded its activities and the files were stored at East India House; there must have been a small army of clerks to keep and maintain the records. When the Company ceased its trading activities there was a huge destruction of those records which were not considered to be of lasting value, including mercantile documents such as cargo manifests and minutes of the Committee of Shipping.

As far as the ships' logs were concerned, however, it was the practice for the captain to hand in his journal, or a copy of it, at the end of each voyage, and most of these important archives have survived, together with the pay-books and wage ledgers.[1] Later in the nineteenth century the neatly written fair copies of the journals were bound at the India Office in London, and they can now be consulted in the Asian & African Studies Reading Room at the British Library.

The journal for each voyage of each ship contains an immense amount of detail. On the first page is the captain's statement that he has given the certificates of good conduct to his officers, and this is followed by a list of the crew members and any passengers who sailed on the ship. The main part of the journal is a day-to-day account of the voyage, starting from when the cargo was taken on board in the docks on the River Thames. It includes the details of course, latitude, longitude and wind direction throughout each day of the voyage, references to significant events which occurred, what cargo was unloaded and loaded in India or China, and a similar detailed account of the long voyage back to England.

VOYAGES OF WILLIAM RIX BLAKELY OF THE HONOURABLE EAST INDIA COMPANY

Ship	Captain	Departure from England	Destination	Return to England	William Rix Blakely's rank
Earl Camden 1,271 tons	Henry Morse Samson	21 January 1810	Bombay and China	[Burnt in Bombay Harbour 23 July 1810]	5th Officer
Arniston 1,200 tons	Samuel Landon	21 January 1810	Bombay and China	13 August 1811	4th Officer

Coutts 1,451 tons	John Boyce	4 January 1812	Bombay and China	8 June 1813	3rd Officer
Coutts 1,451 tons	John Boyce	9 April 1814	China	24 August 1815	3rd Officer
General Hewitt 898 tons	Walter Campbell	9 February 1816	China	12 May 1817	4th Officer
Canning 1,326 tons	William Patterson	31 December 1817	Bombay and China	3 May 1819	2nd Officer
Canning 1,326 tons	William Patterson	4 March 1820	St Helena, Bombay and China	8 June 1821	2nd Officer
Scaleby Castle 1,242 tons	David Rae Newall	18 August 1821	China	10 October 1822	1st Officer
Scaleby Castle 1,242 tons	David Rae Newall	15 March 1823	Bombay and China	5 May 1824	1st Officer
Scaleby Castle 1,242 tons	David Rae Newall	19 February 1825	Bengal and China	17 May 1826	1st Officer
Waterloo 1,325 tons	William Manning	18 March 1827	Madras and China	4 April 1828	1st Officer
Waterloo 1,325 tons	David Rae Newall	30 April 1829	China	30 August 1830	1st Officer
Waterloo 1,325 tons	William Rix Blakely	20 April 1831	China	26 February 1832	Captain
Waterloo 1,325 tons	William Rix Blakely	18 May 1833	China	23 March 1834	Captain

WILLIAM'S FIRST VOYAGE
AS AN OFFICER

Many of those who sailed with the East India Company as officers followed the same progression of promotion. Some, like William, would have started as midshipmen or else saw service in the Royal Navy before transferring to the Company, where they often began as junior officers, perhaps fourth, fifth or even sixth officer in some of the larger ships, and gradually worked their way upwards if they continued with their employment.

The accompanying table gives details of the whole of William's career with the East India Company.[2] He was appointed to an officer's position in the East India Company sometime in 1809, when he was only sixteen. At that time it was quite usual for young potential officers to be given responsibility, and he was appointed fifth officer on the East Indiaman *Earl Camden*.[3] On 21 January 1810 he sailed from Portsmouth, bound for Bombay and China. The *Earl Camden* was on her fourth voyage, having been launched in 1802; the captain was Henry Morse Samson, born at Dover in 1774, who was making his third voyage as captain of this ship; later he was a principal managing owner.

The other ships in the fleet were the *Arniston*, the *Wexford* and the *Winchelsea*, with the *Ocean* going to St Helena and Bencoolen and then to China.[4] The route followed by the ships on the outward voyage was down the English Channel, across the Bay of Biscay, then south-south-westwards towards South America before turning east to go round the Cape of Good Hope, where the fleet anchored on 9 April. The fleet had been escorted by a naval ship, HMS *Illustrious*, although there were complaints from the naval authorities that some East India commanders refused to sail in convoy with a naval escort.[5] A north-easterly course was then followed across the Indian Ocean to India, where they arrived at Bombay on 26 May.

The fleet spent eleven weeks anchored in Bombay, unloading and loading their cargo, before sailing for Penang in Malaya. But they sailed without the *Earl Camden*, for on the night of 22–23 July that ship was burnt in Bombay Harbour. Fire was always a hazard in sailing ships, particularly so when they were on the open seas and little could then be done. The ship had just completed loading a cargo of cotton amounting to 6,000 bales when the fire started in the gun-room. Before long the whole ship was ablaze and she had to be cut from her moorings so that the flood tide could take her away from the rest of the shipping, while the crew took to the boats and escaped without loss of life. The value of the cargo lost was £34,000, a vast sum which gives an indication of the wealth of the East India Company, but payment of the seamen's wages was dependent on the safe arrival of the cargo, and they would have received only a month's pay for the six months' voyage. The subsequent inquiry by the Board of Trade concluded that the fire was the result of "spontaneous ignition", and some recommendations were made about the safe storage of substances containing oil and the stowage of cotton in the hold.[6] William Blakely was fortunate in being transferred to another ship in the same fleet, the *Arniston*.

The *Arniston* and the other two remaining ships, the *Wexford* and the *Winchelsea,* sailed from Bombay on 12 August and reached Penang on 1 September. From there they continued south-eastwards and rounded the southern extremity of the Malay Peninsula before changing course to a little east of north to head for China. At the port of Macao it was the practice for ships to engage Chinese pilots to guide them nearly forty miles to the mouth of the Pearl River (also known as the Canton River). From there it was another twenty-five miles to Whampoa, where a large number of ships from many different countries would be at anchor. As well as being guided by the pilots, the captains used James Horsburgh's *India Directory*, which gave very detailed directions for navigating upstream through the channels.[7]

Cargo for Canton was unloaded at the Whampoa anchorage under the very strict supervision of the Chinese officials, and other cargo, mainly tea, for the return voyage was then taken on board. It was usual for the ships to remain in the vicinity of Whampoa for about four months, but crews had to remain on board ship or on the islands, where the authorities tried to separate different nationalities from brawling with each other. There was plenty for the men to do in making repairs to the ships and cleaning everything thoroughly in preparation for the long voyage home, but they nevertheless became bored and were often ill-behaved.

During this time the captains left the ships to carry out the necessary Company business in Canton and also to arrange their own private business. All officers were allowed to take "private trade" goods on both outward and homeward voyages: captains were allowed as much as 56 tons outward and 38 tons homeward, with much lower amounts available to other officers, midshipmen and some of the seamen who had specific jobs, such as carpenters and cooks.[8] Some captains made considerable profits by this means, and when they retired they were able to live in comfort and great affluence. In Canton the captains stayed with the men of the Select Committee, or Supercargoes, who lived in luxury while representing the East India Company in China and who also made personal fortunes.

On 18 November 1810, while the fleet was making preparations for the voyage back to England, William Blakely received his appointment as fourth officer on the *Arniston*. This ship was similar to the *Earl Camden*, but older and on her seventh voyage. In late December they sailed downstream to the Second Bar, another anchorage where they remained for several weeks, being occupied with further preparations and loading of cargo, until they left China in mid February 1811.

The depleted fleet was joined by four more ships, the *Elphinstone*, the *Cuffnells*, the *Woodford* and the *Alfred* for the homeward voyage. The usual landing was made at St Helena at the end of May, and the *Arniston* finally docked at Long Reach, near Gravesend, on 13 August, where her cargo was unloaded and the crew received their wages. As fourth officer William was paid £2 10s a month, a sum not very different from members of the crew such as the coxswain, the sailmaker and the ship's cook.[9] After unloading was completed William had a few months' leave before joining another ship. The *Arniston*'s next voyage began in January 1812 and was to Bombay and China. Later she was requisitioned as a troopship by the government, but was wrecked off the coast of South Africa in 1815 on her homeward voyage from Ceylon and almost all the 378 passengers and crew were lost.

AN ADMINISTRATIVE PROBLEM

During his leave William went to Knapton where his family was now living following the death of his father in June 1810. He had probably heard about this through the efficiency of the East India Company, which enabled letters to reach ships during their voyages. Before the end of 1811 his next voyage had been arranged: he was to sail as third officer on the *Coutts*, again to Bombay and China. The *Coutts* was another large vessel on her seventh voyage and her captain, John Boyce, was making his second voyage as the ship's commander. William's appointment was a promotion, but it brought with it an administrative problem which was to return many years later.

Since the end of the eighteenth century regulations had

been laid down by the East India Company concerning the age and experience of those appointed as officers. The regulations in force in 1811 required third officers to be at least twenty-one years old and to have completed two voyages to India or China, and fourth officers to be twenty years old with one voyage to India or China.[10] When William was appointed fourth officer on the *Arniston* he had presumably completed at least one voyage as a midshipman, but he was not then required to produce evidence of his age. It may be assumed that this was because the appointment was made in China after the fire destroyed the *Earl Camden*. He was prepared to affirm that he was aged twenty, having been born in 1790. Whether he really believed this to be true (it will be recalled that he was born in 1793) is not known, but when he was about to be appointed third officer on the *Coutts* he was required to produce evidence of his age. These are his own words:

> I wrote home for a certificate and received for answer there was no age attached to the Baptismal register and that my name was not William Rix but Willm Martin but that I was born in 1790 and upon this without further enquiry I made the wrong affirmation.[11]

This quite extraordinary state of affairs arose from the fact that in the Thrandeston church register the record of the public baptism of William and his elder brother Thomas on 1 August 1793 is incorrectly given, their second names having been interchanged. It is stated that "Thomas Rix" Blakely was privately baptised on 25 April 1790 and "William Martin" was privately baptised on 8 May 1793. Despite this apparent evidence, why William's mother was not able to tell him his proper name and the correct year of his birth is a mystery, but his affirmed age of twenty-one in 1811 was accepted. He must have been one of the youngest third officers to serve with the East India Company being, in fact, only eighteen years of age. He was, nevertheless, always known as William Rix Blakely in the Company's records.

OTHER EARLY VOYAGES

At this time in the early nineteenth century Britain was at war, and even merchant ships were liable to be attacked. In 1810 the East Indiaman *Ceylon* had been captured by the French in the Indian Ocean and taken to Mauritius. Later she was retaken by the British and sailed back to England in company with the *Arniston*, on which William was fourth officer. On board the *Ceylon*, also as fourth officer, was David Rae Newall, a Scot from Dumfries, with whom William was to make four voyages later in his career. In 1812 Britain was at war with the United States and, to save expense on naval vessels, many merchant ships sailed as privateers: that is, they were authorised by the government to attack enemy shipping. The *Coutts* was one of these, although as the letter of marque giving authority to attack American ships was issued when the ship was in China, it is unlikely that any such action took place.[12]

William's next two voyages were both as third officer on the *Coutts* with John Boyce as captain. The first was to Bombay and China and the second was only to China. The East India Company ships' voyages were arranged in annual seasons and, as each voyage took up to eighteen months, any one officer or seaman usually sailed in alternate seasons. This gave them an extended period of leave in between, and William would have been able to visit his family in Norfolk at that time.

Communication between people in different parts of the world was a long, drawn-out process 200 years ago and in 1816 the British government decided to send an embassy to the court of Peking in China, in order to persuade the Chinese authorities to remove some of the restrictions which they imposed on European traders. The embassy was financed by the East India Company, which sent one of their ships, the *General Hewitt*, to accompany the Royal Navy frigate *Alceste* and the brig *Lyra*. The leader of the delegation was Lord Amherst, who sailed with his suite on the *Alceste*, while one of the functions of the *General Hewitt* was to carry the presents to be given to the Emperor of China.

William Blakely was appointed fourth officer on the *General Hewitt* and the three ships sailed from Portsmouth on 9 February 1816. It was not very usual for an officer to have his rank lowered, but there was not much difference in pay between the junior officers, and this voyage gave William the opportunity of seeing a part of China which few Europeans had ever visited. The three ships spent about two weeks in port at the Cape of Good Hope, where the *Alceste* had arrived a few days after the other two, having paid a visit to Rio de Janeiro. Although the *Alceste* left the Cape ten days after the *General Hewitt* and the *Lyra* she was a faster ship and sailed across the Indian Ocean to arrive at the next port, Batavia on the island of Java, on 9 June, only two days later than the others. In July a call was made at Hong Kong in order to pick up other diplomats and interpreters.[13] They then sailed up the coast to the Yellow Sea and the Gulf of Pe-tche-lee where, early in August, the presents were off-loaded from the *General Hewitt* and the members of the embassy disembarked to travel to Peking, a distance of about 100 miles.

The main object of the diplomatic mission failed, owing to Lord Amherst being advised not to perform the ceremony of kowtow to the Emperor. The story was later narrated in fine detail by some members of the delegation.[14] The party eventually made its way by land and river to Canton, a journey which took four months, while the *General Hewitt* took just a month to sail to Canton. The crew of that ship would have been aware of some of the political problems, as the Chinese authorities tried to prevent them from loading their return cargo of tea at Canton. In due course the difficulties were overcome and they set sail for England at the beginning of December, reaching the River Thames on 12 May 1817. Lord Amherst and his companions were not so fortunate. On their return the *Alceste* was wrecked on an uncharted reef off the coast of Sumatra: the account of their rescue and return to England was included in the published narratives.

For his next two voyages William was promoted to second officer on the *Canning*, going to Bombay and China. Clearly he was an able officer who carried out his duties responsibly. He returned to England at the beginning of June 1821, when he progressed further up the promotion ladder.

WILLIAM BECOMES FIRST OFFICER

Although most officers, seamen and ships usually sailed in alternate seasons, two men had a very short period of leave between voyages in 1821: these were David Newall and William Blakely. Newall had been first officer on the *General Hewitt*, which returned to England at the end of May, and he was then appointed captain of the *Scaleby Castle*, which was to set sail in mid August. William was appointed to be his first officer. It has not been established whether the two men had previously known each other, although they might have met in 1811 on their return voyages to England. They sailed together as captain and first officer four times between 1821 and 1830, each voyage taking about fifteen months.

The *Scaleby Castle* had been built in Bombay in 1798 and was formerly in private trade to India as a licensed ship. By 1834 she had made fourteen voyages in the service of the East India

Company. This was more than any other of the Company's ships, and well beyond the maximum of eight voyages which was previously laid down in the regulations.[15] The voyage which started in 1821 was her eighth for the Company, and was unusual in that the ship sailed very late in the season and was not accompanied by any other East Indiamen.[16]

Like the two senior officers, the ship had not long returned from her previous voyage and perhaps needed little in the way of repairs before her next one. They sailed from the Downs, the area off the east coast of Kent where the fleet usually gathered, on 18 August, and did not make any landfall until they reached China on 21 January 1822. This outward voyage was much longer than normal on account of the course which they followed.[17] They took the usual route across the Atlantic Ocean until winds were picked up which took them east to go round the Cape of Good Hope early in November. Because of the lateness of the season they maintained an easterly course further than was customary, passing about fifteen miles to the south of the remote, uninhabited island of St Paul. By the beginning of December, having turned north-east, they were about 200 miles from the north-west coast of Australia.

In the ship's log it is recorded that at 8.30 p.m. on 5 December the ship hove to and the cutter was sent ahead to look out for Cloates Island or the Tryal Rocks. The existence of this island and reef had long puzzled mariners and Captain Newall, believing his ship to be in their vicinity, wanted to avoid the risk of the ship running into them, especially at night. It is probable that the chart they were using marked possible locations for these potential hazards: one such chart had been published for the East India Company by George Robertson in 1790.[18] The ship's cutter was manned by a midshipman, a quartermaster and six seamen, but the investigation had a tragic outcome, for the cutter was never seen again.

It so happened that Captain Newall was ill and unable to

take command of the search for the boat and its crew. The responsibility therefore devolved on to First Officer Blakely. The officers and men made a thorough search lasting a whole day and night, and they fired guns and burnt blue lights to try to attract the attention of the missing boat. But, after questioning the crew and taking advice from his fellow officers, William finally conceded that some misfortune had come upon the vessel and they had to continue without their shipmates. This accident resulted in the greatest loss of life that William encountered on any of his voyages, and it illustrates some of the dangers which mariners faced. The incident was reported briefly in an English newspaper, but not until the *Scaleby Castle* was nearing the end of her voyage in October 1822.[19]

In the early nineteenth century longitude was determined by astronomical methods, dead reckoning and chronometers, but the position of a ship could be wrong by several degrees, especially after sailing for weeks without seeing any land. Much later it was found that Cloates "Island" is part of the mainland of Australia and the Tryal Rocks are north-west of the Monte Bello Islands group; both are further east than where the *Scaleby Castle* was at the time.

After this incident the *Scaleby Castle* continued north-eastwards and then north to negotiate what are now known as the islands of Indonesia. Horsburgh's chart of the Eastern Passages to China had not yet been published, so they were dependent on earlier charts to find their way. Having passed north of the island of Timor, they crossed the Banda Sea and entered an area called the Pitt Passage. From several possible routes towards the Pacific Ocean they chose the Gillolo Passage. Later, Horsburgh wrote in his *India Directory* that:

> many persons prefer the Gillolo Passage, for the following reasons: it is spacious, the islands on each side are bold to approach, and clear of hidden danger,

there is good room for working by night or by day, and
the tides or currents in it are seldom strong.[20]

It seems likely that, despite the Gillolo Passage having been
used for some time as a route leading to the Pacific Ocean,
charts were incomplete when the *Scaleby Castle* went that way
in December 1821. For, while traversing the passage, William
made observations of their course, recording also the bearings
of the islands which they passed. His readings are in the ship's
log, which is particularly detailed for the four days that the
passage took. When the ship was anchored in China early
in 1822, or perhaps when he returned to England, he drew
a chart of the course and adjacent islands and illustrated it
with ten drawings of some of the islands. The chart was then
engraved and published by the East India Company in 1823,
price 2s 0d.[21]

The remainder of the voyage to China, in a wide loop to
the east of the Philippines, took three weeks, and the usual
unloading and loading of cargo then took place at Whampoa.
On the return voyage the *Scaleby Castle* followed the more
direct route by way of the Sunda Strait between Java and
Sumatra, and then sailed straight across the Indian Ocean
to go round the southern tip of Africa. As usual a stop was
made at St Helena, where several days were spent in early
August. For the final leg of the voyage from the island back
to England Brigadier General John Pine Coffin and his wife
joined the ship as passengers: this officer had been governor
of St Helena since the return to England of the then governor,
Sir Hudson Lowe, after the death of Napoleon in May 1821.
After leaving the island the *Scaleby Castle* sailed in company
with the chartered ship *Florentia*, which was carrying £500,000
from India for the East India Company. The ships arrived back
in England in October 1822.[22]

In 1823–4 and 1825–6 William again sailed as first officer

with Captain Newall on the *Scaleby Castle*; on both voyages they made calls in India before continuing on to China. Promotion in the Company was by seniority, and William remained first officer longer than some other officers because there were those who had been in the Company longer than he had. As a result he was first officer for a further two voyages: the first with Captain William Manning and the second with Captain Newall, both on the *Waterloo*, a Company ship built in 1816. Between the latter voyages he had a long leave of almost a year: in the summer of 1828 he went on a tour which took in the northern part of Wales, north-west England and Ireland, both north and south. His comments on the sights he saw and the people he met are contained in a letter which he wrote to his brother Edward. An amusing episode occurred when he visited the rope bridge at Carrick-a-Rede on the Antrim coast. Crossing it even today requires a head for heights, but in the early nineteenth century it must have been quite hair-raising. William recorded that he was the only person to make the crossing on the day of his visit, and he was "fool hardy enough to take off [his] hat in the middle and give three cheers much to the horror of the lookers on".

A LONG DETENTION AND
ITS CONSEQUENCES

Between January 1829 and the beginning of June twenty-two East India ships left England for China. The majority went to India first, but five were scheduled for "China direct", two of which were the *Scaleby Castle* and the *Waterloo*. At the end of April the *Waterloo* sailed from the River Thames, captained by David Newall with William Blakely as his first officer.[23] It was a voyage which was considerably longer than planned, and one in which there were problems over discipline in some of the ships in the fleet. The outward journey passed mainly without incident. As usual they anchored briefly in Anjer Roads in the Sunda Strait off the island of Java, where fresh water and other supplies were taken on board. There was also the opportunity to send letters back to England if there was a ship at the anchorage which could take them. They soon set sail again on the final leg of the voyage, and on the evening of 31 August the *Waterloo* anchored in Macao Roads, where inbound ships stopped to await the pilot to guide them up the Pearl River. But this time things were different.

Trade between Britain and China had flourished for many years under the East India Company and was of economic benefit to both countries. Cloth, woollens, iron and other goods were exported to China, and in return China sold porcelain, silk and, above all, tea to Britain. At Canton trading had to be arranged between the Select Committee and the Hong merchants who were appointed by the Chinese authorities. In 1829 the Committee decided to ban trading in order to force the Chinese authorities to address their complaints: the main ones were that the number of Hong merchants had been reduced as a result of bankruptcies and that high port charges were levied on ships at Whampoa.[24] The Committee used the excuse of danger to the health of the crews from malaria and dysentery to stop the incoming fleet from sailing up the river to Whampoa to unload until the authorities acceded to their demands. By the middle of October there were twenty ships at anchor in Toon-koo Bay and Cap-sing-moon Bay, near Hong Kong Island, waiting to sail upstream to unload.

This political move on the part of the Committee understandably frustrated the officers and men of the ships of the fleet. Towards the end of November William sent a letter to his brother Edward in which he wrote:

When we are again to be in England I cannot at this present time give you the least notion of for the fleet is all detained outside the port of Canton. ... We amuse ourselves in the fleet as we best can with boat racing, shooting excursions, and one thing with another the time as yet has not been very heavy on our hands. However long faces and deep groans are occasionally seen and heard as the time advances.

Shortly after this William was able to leave the *Waterloo* in order to carry out a survey of the channels leading to the Lymoon, the narrow passage between Hong Kong Island and the mainland. He took with him other officers from the *Waterloo*, the *Buckinghamshire*, the *Atlas* and the *Scaleby Castle*, and seamen to row them around in the ships' boats. The survey took them about ten days to complete.

William undertook a second survey later in December, but this time the *Waterloo* moved from her position in Toon-koo Bay and anchored some fourteen miles further up the river estuary. The survey, conducted by the same officers as before, was of the channel to the east of Fansyack. It also took about ten days, and on New Year's Day 1830 the ship returned to her anchorage near the other ships of the fleet. Charts drawn from the two surveys were published by the Company in 1830. The results of the surveys were incorporated into Horsburgh's *India Directory* and his chart of the Canton River, where William's contributions were acknowledged. After the ship had returned to England the officers who had done the surveys were presented with surveying instruments by the Company for their "meritorious services ... in making accurate surveys". William received a six-inch theodolite.[25]

The Company had a house in Macao which was home to the Company's resident officials. This was used by some of the ships' captains for social purposes and as a means of avoiding the tedious conditions on board their ships. As the distance between the anchorage at Toon-koo Bay and Macao is nearly thirty miles, the captains must have left command of the ships to their first officers for a considerable period of time. Evidence for this is found in the diary of Harriett Low, a young American lady who lived with her aunt Abigail in Macao for four years between 1829 and 1833. She wrote about parties, plays and balls which she attended and mentioned several captains by name. These included Captain Newall, who paid her many visits, one being on the day after the *Waterloo* had rejoined the rest of the fleet at the beginning of January.[26] The ships' logs are more terse, with phrases like "Captain – left the ship for Macao", and "Captain – joined the ship".

But the ordinary seamen could indulge in no such pleasures. In some of the ships there were problems over discipline, and conditions on the *Scaleby Castle* were particularly difficult. On the voyage to China Captain James Burnett was clearly having problems with his crew. It was the first time he had been captain, and it seems as though he was not able to maintain discipline. Before reaching the Cape there had been an incident, which was later the subject of an action in the Court of Common Pleas, in which Burnett was fined £50 for mistreating a marine boy.[27]

In late December the captain went to Macao, and during his absence there was a disturbance on board his ship: a seaman had used disrespectful language to the gunner and refused to do any duty until the captain returned. The captain was summoned back, but when he arrived three days later and ordered the man to be flogged, the quartermasters refused to obey the captain's orders. The ship's log records that it "Made signal No. 369 [the signal for a mutiny] which was promptly answered by every ship near us sending armed boats".[28]

William and his fellow officers on the *Waterloo* were not among those who helped to quell the mutiny as their ship was still further up the river where the survey was being conducted, but they would have been well aware of the situation when they rejoined the fleet: four of the miscreants from the *Scaleby Castle* were transferred to the *Waterloo* for the remainder of the voyage in China and back to England. It is clear that Captain Newall, assisted by First Officer Blakely and others, ran a well-ordered ship in which the crew were much happier than in several other ships. On the voyage back to England there was another mutiny, on board the *Inglis*. Back in England in the autumn of 1830, Captain Burnett, the captains of the *General Kyd*, the *Lowther Castle* and the *Inglis* and the first officer of the *Inglis* were taken to court by men from their ships.[29] Even though all the officers were acquitted, these cases were indicative of unrest in some parts of fleet.

The fleet remained at the anchorages at Toon-koo Bay and Cap-sing-moon Bay for about a month after the mutiny on the *Scaleby Castle*, but eventually Harriett Low was able to write in her diary that:

> The Company have decided all their difficulties with the Chinese, and the Ships are all ordered to Whampoa Chop Chop. The Capt's. are all off, and many happy hearts and smiling faces are the consequences. They have all been very anxious to get away.[30]

The ships then proceeded upstream to unload their cargoes and to begin loading cargo for the return voyage. These operations at Whampoa were completed by the end of March and the fleet was able to begin the long voyage back to England.

But the problems which had arisen in China were not yet over. The mutiny on the *Inglis* occurred on 6 June off the Cape of Good Hope and this, together with disturbances on some of the other ships, resulted in a court of inquiry being held on St Helena when the ships were in port there. The court was convened by the governor of the island and, having dealt with the seamen, he ordered seven ships to proceed under convoy back to England accompanied by the frigate HMS *Ariadne*. Christopher Biden wrote that:

> The anomalous state of the merchant-service has been brought to a crisis, by the unprecedented occurrence of a fleet of Company's ships being sent, under convoy, from the island of St. Helena to England, during a season of profound peace.[31]

The departure of the convoy from St Helena in July 1830 was illustrated in a splendid picture by the East India Company artist W.J. Huggins, shown in Plate 7. The East Indiamen *Inglis*, *Windsor*, *Waterloo*, *Scaleby Castle*, *General Kyd*, *Farquharson* and *Lowther Castle*, together with HMS *Ariadne*, are shown in full sail with the island in the background. Huggins had made only one voyage to India and China as a seaman and all his work was produced in London, but his paintings are authentic regarding their detail.[32]

The ships reached the shores of England at the end of August and the officers and crews dispersed, some for a well-earned rest but others to prepare for their appearances in court. It had been a particularly difficult sixteen months.

CAPTAIN BLAKELY

After this voyage William had reached the point of being the Company's most senior first officer and was therefore due for promotion to captain when a vacancy arose. There were, in fact, quite a number of changes among the captains for the following season. Among these, William's friend David Newall retired from the Company's service and Captain Burnett of

East India Company fleet leaving St Helena, July 1830. By W.J. Huggins
Image © National Maritime Museum, Greenwich, London
Plate 7

the *Scaleby Castle* wrote to the Company asking to be appointed captain of the *Waterloo* in his place: rather presumptuously, it might be thought, as only the previous week Burnett had asked the Company to pay the legal expenses for his defence against a charge of ill treatment of one of those responsible for the mutiny in China. Nevertheless, at their meeting on 13 October 1830, the Court of Directors approved his appointment as captain of the *Waterloo* and William Rix Blakely was promoted to command the *Scaleby Castle* for the following season. A week later William attended the court to be duly sworn in as captain, and the arrangements for the ensuing voyage to China were made, to set sail in the spring of 1831. But in the middle of November Captain Burnett wrote again to the Company to make a formal request to stay at home for the forthcoming season on the grounds of ill health. Although he was able to produce the required medical certificates, the real reason must have been his trial for ill-treating Quartermaster Thomas Lamb. At the same time William asked to be transferred to the *Waterloo*, and both of these requests were granted at the meeting of the court on 1 December. Both the *Scaleby Castle* and the *Waterloo* were Company ships and consequently several other changes were made for senior officers, including John Hillman being promoted to command the *Scaleby Castle*.[33] Hillman had been first officer of the *Buckinghamshire* in the preceding season and would have known all about the problems which beset some of the ships. His captain on that voyage was Richard Glasspoole, an East Anglian like William, who described him as "looking fat and well and collecting all kinds of natural curiosities for the Norwich Museum".[34]

William's first journey to China as captain of the *Waterloo* was uneventful in comparison with his previous voyage.[35] On 5 March 1831 he was on board the ship with some of his officers in the East India Export dock at Blackwall on the Thames. At the end of March the ship moved downstream to

Gravesend, where loading of the cargo began. The Company's cargo was iron and bales of woollen material. Loading this, together with the officers' private trade goods and all necessary food, water and other essentials for 150 people for more than three months, took about three weeks.

On 12 April Captain Blakely formally took leave of the Court of Directors of the Company at East India House. At last all was ready, four passengers came on board with their baggage, and they set sail on 21 April. Two days later they were off the Lizard Point and left England behind. The usual course and routine were followed as the days and weeks went by. Every Sunday while at sea it was part of the captain's responsibility to conduct divine service for the ship's company and if, for any reason, he did not do so then an explanation had to be entered in the log.[36] William was quite conscientious in this respect but there were a number of occasions when the service did not take place. The most common reason was that the weather was too cold or too windy, but sometimes it was "the necessary duty of the ship" that prevented him from taking the service.

The distance travelled each day was very dependent on winds, currents and the weather, but the *Waterloo* was one of the fastest East Indiamen of her time. On a typical day they might cover up to 200 miles or even more: in 1830 a former captain of the *Waterloo*, Richard Alsager, had said in evidence to a House of Lords Committee regarding the affairs of the East India Company that:

The *Waterloo* is a very fast-sailing Ship. I have been in Company with Vessels of War, and we made a very good Figure; we like a good strong Breeze. I came Home in Twenty-one Days from the Line, and we averaged 200 Miles, and I have run 260 Miles by Observation; it is not a bad-sailing Ship which can do that.[37]

The *Waterloo* reached her first landfall on the island of Java in mid July and anchored there for a short while in order to replenish the supply of fresh water. They then set sail again and on 31 July reached Macao Roads, where the passengers disembarked and preparations began for moving to Whampoa to unload the cargo. Even though there were no restrictions such as were endured two years earlier, it was nevertheless quite a time before they were allowed to sail up the Pearl River: they moved their anchorage to the Second Bar on 7 August and it was another two weeks before the final stage took them to Whampoa.

Unloading the Company's cargo of iron and bales of woollen goods and officers' private trade material took about three weeks, and they then began to load boxes of tea for the return voyage to England. William spent part of this time in Canton, staying with members of the Select Committee and attending to the necessary documentation for the trading. By 18 October all was ready: they sailed the short distance to Macao, where two Chinese students embarked as passengers, and then set sail for England in company with the *Buckinghamshire*, captained by William's friend Richard Glasspoole.

The log records that on 3 January 1832, as they were approaching St Helena, it was necessary to shift 200 chests of tea from the starboard to the larboard (port) side of the ship in order to keep her on an even keel. As was customary the ship called at St Helena, after which an unusual entry was made in the log for Sunday 29 January: "desired Mr. Allchin Chief Officer to consider himself under arrest for unofficerlike Conduct on the Saturday night."

While no indication is given of what Thomas Allchin had done, a reasonable supposition is that he was drunk. His only child, a daughter, was born on 5 November 1831 and it is just possible that a letter from his wife might have reached St Helena before the arrival of the *Waterloo* nine weeks later. As there is no further reference to the episode it is likely that no more action was taken. An incident like this could have cost Allchin his job, but William did give him his certificate of good conduct at the end of the voyage. Nevertheless, in the following season Thomas Allchin sailed on the *Scaleby Castle* as first officer under John Hillman, with whom he had previously sailed on several voyages, rather than with William, who perhaps did not want him again as his first officer.

The end of the *Waterloo*'s voyage was now approaching: the lighthouse at the Lizard Point was sighted on 18 February and they anchored in the Downs in thick fog a week later. It remained for the cargo to be unloaded in the docks, and on 31 March William signed off his log after a successful voyage.

WILLIAM'S LAST VOYAGE TO CHINA

After nearly a year's leave William was ready to start on what was to be his last voyage to China. It was also the last voyage of the *Waterloo*, as the East India Company's trading operations ceased in 1834. The usual preparations began on 18 March 1833 and a month later the ship was towed downstream to the loading anchorage at Northfleet, at which time Captain Blakely was summoned to East India House to take leave of the Court of Directors. Eventually everything was ready and they sailed from the Downs on 18 May.[38] On the outward journey there were ten passengers, including two Supercargoes who were going to Canton. Between England and Java the log records that five other vessels were seen, two of which were travelling towards England, and the opportunity was taken of passing some letters to them which they would take to England. When other ships were seen it was common practice to "speak" to them by means of signal flags, and by this means news of ships' progress was often reported in the newspapers.

Some eight weeks after leaving England the captain's

cook died and was buried at sea: deaths on the long voyages were not uncommon, especially among the seamen whose health was often affected by poor living conditions on board. Nevertheless, when they reached Anjer Roads in the middle of August to replenish supplies, William was able to send a letter to his brother Edward, in which he said that he had "enjoyed good health and been extremely happy and comfortable with my passengers, my Officers and Ship's Company, and have every prospect of continuing so". He also wrote that he had bought a quantity of Straits produce – rattans and rice, according to the log – as part of his captain's private trade allowance, and would therefore remain at Anjer for a day or two longer than planned. The final stage of the voyage to Macao took another eighteen days, during which time they were accompanied by the East Indiaman *Minerva*, which had left England twelve days earlier than the *Waterloo*.

The ship arrived off Macao on 6 September, where the passengers disembarked and the ship lay at anchor, but moving her position a little in the wide estuary, for nearly three weeks. Towards the end of this time Captain William left the ship to go to Canton, and on 25 September they began to move up the Pearl River to Whampoa. There the familiar routine of unloading the Company's cargo and private trade goods took place, and then chests of tea for the return voyage were loaded. The captain's own cargo to take back to England included some partridge canes and chinaware.

An entry in the log for 12 October states that they sent their launch to the assistance of the *Warren Hastings*, which had grounded in the Pearl River near the Second Bar. Perhaps as a mark of gratitude the *Warren Hastings* gave the *Waterloo* some "shore bread", but on the following day it was found that it was too bad to eat and it was condemned. By the third week in November all was ready for the long voyage back across the oceans, and they sailed down the river in company with the

Farquharson and anchored off Macao to receive the dispatches for the Company in London and for some passengers to go aboard, one of whom was the young lady Harriett Low.

Mention has been made earlier of Harriett, who was living in Macao with her aunt Abigail. They had sailed from Massachusetts in 1829 when Harriett's uncle, William Low, had the opportunity to go to Canton on business. As Western women were not allowed to live in Canton, Harriett went as a companion to her aunt while her husband was away. Towards the end of 1833 William Low's health was very poor, caused partly by overwork, and he was advised by his doctor to leave China as soon as possible in the hope that a long voyage would enable him to recover. He was, in fact, suffering from consumption, as tuberculosis was then called. Mr Low accordingly made arrangements for himself, his wife and Harriett to travel to England on the *Waterloo*, and the family, together with their Chinese servant and two other men, were the passengers who joined the ship at Macao. Harriett wrote in her diary almost daily, so it is possible to read a first-hand account of what life was like on an East Indiaman under the command of Captain Blakely, whom she described as "an excellent man and a man of talents".[39]

Accommodation for the captain and his passengers was comparatively luxurious, and the Low family had their own cabins and ate their meals with the captain and his senior officers. Harriett spent much of her time reading, eating and sleeping, although she suffered badly from sea-sickness when gales were blowing. Ten days after leaving Macao they approached the Banca Strait, a narrow channel between the islands of Banca (Bangka) and Sumatra. This was quite often used in preference to the more direct, but equally hazardous, Gaspar Strait.

Navigation in the Banca Strait was not easy as there were hidden rocks and, at the southern end, a dangerous shoal where many ships had grounded. These included the *Waterloo* on her maiden voyage in 1817, when she was immobile for nine days and had to transfer some of her guns and cargo to the *Winchelsea* before she could be refloated.[40] On this occasion, however, Captain Blakely took the precaution of anchoring overnight and for some shorter periods, as the weather alternated between calm and squalls of rain with thunderstorms. Eventually they were clear of the channel and in the open sea, sailing towards Anjer on Java. They reached Anjer on 6 December and anchored there for the night, having replenished their supplies of water, fresh meat and fruit. William had hoped to pick up some more passengers, and was disappointed to find that there were none.

The long passage across the Indian Ocean then began, with very little to interest the passengers apart from the ship itself. When he was able to leave the running of the ship to his officers William took time to talk with his passengers, and Harriett found the conversations stimulating. She also records that she played many games of backgammon with him. Her uncle's health was not improving, even with the fine weather, and the advice from one of the other passengers, a Royal Navy doctor, was that he should not go further than St Helena. William Low, however, was of the opinion that both climate and accommodation would be better at the Cape of Good Hope. The ship was not due to call there but Captain Blakely was glad of an excuse to do so, and thought he would probably be able to agree to the request. In due course he consulted his fellow officers, who agreed that it would be a sensible change of plan, and they reached the Cape on 13 January 1834, having made excellent progress with as much as 254 miles being sailed on one particularly good day.[41] The Low family disembarked and found places to stay in South Africa. Sadly, though, William Low's health gradually declined further and he died on 22 March, aged only thirty-eight. His widow and niece eventually made their way to England on the

Royal George and then had a very rough passage back to America.

Meanwhile the *Waterloo* continued on her voyage, stopping as usual at St Helena from 25 to 28 January, where the anchors and cables were inspected. They then made sail to pass near Ascension Island and, later, the Azores before reaching the English Channel. After passing Lizard Point they hove to while the first pilot came on board and after they sighted Dungeness Lighthouse the Deal pilot boarded the ship to guide her towards the Thames estuary. The River pilot came on board for the final stage of the voyage to the moorings and on 29 March the ship's company was discharged, having received their pay. The last entry in the log was made on 25 April to record the arrival of His Majesty's Customs officers. So ended the ninth and final voyage of the *Waterloo*. The East India Company's trading business had now ceased and, like some of the other East Indiamen, the vessel was sold to ship-breakers. By December 1834 demolition was complete.

WILLIAM'S RETIREMENT IN SUFFOLK

Officers in the East India Company maritime service had lonely jobs, especially the more senior men, with no one to talk to apart from those on the ship, and it is not surprising that some found it difficult to settle at home on leave or in retirement. This perhaps explains why William never married, but he was friendly with the families of some of his fellow officers. One of these was Philip Baylis. The two men were never on the same ship together, although they were both in China in the autumn of 1818 when Philip was second officer on the *Earl of Balcarras* and William had the same rank on the *Canning*. Philip was six years older than William and was born in London; in 1825 he married Mary Ann Clubbe, who was niece of Ann, the wife of Francis Leeke of Yaxley Hall, near

Thrandeston. Mr Leeke was an elderly gentleman who was
friendly with William for many years; he gave him a large tip
when he was about to go off to join his ship, perhaps for the
first time as a midshipman.[42] Later on Mr Leeke appointed
William to be the executor of his will, for which both William
and Philip acted as witnesses.

For many years William shared a house with Philip at
Stoke Ash, a village on the Ipswich to Norwich road not far
from Thrandeston. The house was a moated farmhouse called
Coulsey Wood, which was described by Farrer in his series of
articles *Some Old Houses in Suffolk*.[43] He wrote that Captains
Blakely and Baylis lived in the house alternately when they
were on leave from their voyages, although the Baylis family
would also have been in residence. There were six Baylis
children, the eldest two of whom were named William Rix
and Francis Leeke; William Blakely was godfather to his
namesake and left him a legacy of £50 and his gold watch and
seals. When the captains retired from their maritime service
they continued to live at Coulsey Wood and joined in local
activities, both social and civil.

Another of William's acquaintances was David Charles
Read, an artist who worked mainly as an etcher but who also
painted with the brush. Read was born in Hampshire and
lived for much of his life in the Cathedral Close at Salisbury.
As far as is known he did not live in Suffolk, but one of his
patrons was Chambers Hall, the son of an East India Company
maritime captain whose family was well acquainted with the
Leekes of Yaxley. Read did some work for the Leekes and knew
both William, when he was at Coulsey Wood on leave, and
also his brother Edward, who was establishing himself in the
shawl trade in Norwich. A catalogue of Read's etchings was
published in 1832 which included the names of purchasers,
three of whom were Captain Blakely, E. Blakely and Mrs
Leeke of Yaxley Hall. Among the eighty-seven prints which

were etched between 1827 and 1831 is one of Calshot Castle, which was dedicated to Captain Blakely.[44] The inscription below the print reads:

To my Active Friend Captain Blakely – David C. Read.
Close Salisbury March 1831.

This date was just before William left for China on the first of his voyages as captain. At the same time Read painted a large portrait of him in his captain's uniform.

Most officers in the East India Company took advantage of the private trade arrangements, in particular bringing quantities of material home from the Far East to sell, and it is likely that William assisted his brother Edward by bringing home silks from India and China. It is known that the Company ordered large quantities of textiles from Norwich manufacturers for export; these were mainly camlets, which were rolls of fabric made from worsted.[45] Edward was not a manufacturer of camlets, but it is quite possible that William was able to sell some of Edward's goods for him, either as Company trades or as part of his private trade allowance.

The Company looked after its officers, and many retired on generous pensions. Some, especially the captains, made considerable fortunes. It is doubtful if William was extremely wealthy, although his will does indicate that he was quite well off. However, his name has not been found in pension lists, possibly because he retired at the very end of the trading operations. But there is also a strong possibility that he had to forego any claim which he might have had because of the muddle over his birth and baptism dates so many years before.

In 1835, in relation to his expected gratuity and pension, he was asked to provide evidence of his age, and in reply he wrote to the secretary to the directors of the Company explaining the problem which had arisen earlier in his career. In his letter he said that he had been to see the rector of Thrandeston who was then in office and found that the last two lines on the page of the church register, which contained the incorrect names of himself and his brother, were written in different handwriting and in much blacker ink than the other entries. He suspected that there had been some deception in the register entries and, although this was not caused by himself, he was willing to bear financial loss by not claiming his pension, rather than have the affair made public. It seems as though he did suffer financially through this error made long before.[46]

William continued to live with the Baylis family at Coulsey Wood until Michaelmas 1842, when they all moved away owing to problems over the poor condition of the house, which was later rebuilt. The Baylises moved to Ipswich and William went to a hotel in Yarmouth, probably for the sake of his health. But he did not have long to live, for on 2 November he died there at the age of forty-nine. The cause of his death was consumption, perhaps brought on by his years at sea. Like many of his ancestors, he was buried in Thrandeston churchyard.

From the evidence that there is about him, William had been a good seaman who rose to top rank through his ability to manage both ship and crew. He had learned much of his craft on the job and was strongly influenced by Captain Newall, with whom he had spent long periods of his life. Newall was described in his obituary as "a genial-hearted English gentleman of the old school".[47] During his sea-going career Newall had managed his crews in a firm yet fair manner, which was by no means always the case in the first part of the nineteenth century, and William Blakely treated the men of his ship in the same way.

CHAPTER FOUR NOTES

1. Anthony Farrington, *Catalogue of East India Company ships' journals and logs, 1600–1834* (British Library, 1999), Introduction. Outline details of the voyages of each ship are also available on the National Archives website at <http://discovery.nationalarchives. gov.uk> under British Library: Asian and African Studies [accessed 23 December 2015].

2. Anthony Farrington, *A Biographical Index of East India Company maritime service officers, 1600–1834* (British Library, 1999). This book has been used to identify the ships on which William served during the first part of his maritime career.

3. "Professional skills were acquired at a much earlier age than in the Company's Armies – twelve or thirteen was normal for a first voyage – and command, given good connections, could come by the mid-twenties." Farrington, *Biographical Index*, Introduction.

4. Charles Hardy, *Register of Ships Employed in the Service of the East India Company from 1760 to 1810* (London, 1811), p. 283. The *Ocean* was lost in the China Seas on or after 5 September 1810. H.B. Morse, *The Chronicles of the East India Company Trading to China 1635–1834*, vol. III (Oxford, 1926), p. 143.

5. Arrival of HMS *Illustrious* with *Wexford*, *Earl Camden*, *Arniston* and *Winchelsea*. Factory Records, Cape of Good Hope, 14 April 1810. BL, IOR/G/9/7, ff. 104–105. Complaint by Vice Admiral Sir Albemarle Bertie on failure of EIC ships to sail with Naval escort in convoy and justification of action by EIC commanders. Factory Records, Cape of Good Hope, 31 March–30 May 1810. BL, IOR/G/9/11, ff. 1–46.

6. E. Samuel, *Asiatic Annual Register*, vol. XII for the Year 1810–11 (London, 1812), pp. 24–5, 137; *Second Report from the Select Committee*

of the House of Commons on the Affairs of the East India Company (London,
1830), p. 978; *Literary Panorama*, vol. X, August 1811 (London, 1811),
col. 336–8; Jean Sutton, *Lords of the East: the East India Company and its
ships (1600–1874)* (London, 2000), p. 80; Jean Sutton, *The East India
Company's Maritime Service 1746–1834* (Woodbridge, 2010), pp. 233,
243 n. 38.

7. James Horsburgh, *The India Directory, or Directions for Sailing to and from
the East Indies, China, Australia, and the Interjacent Ports of Africa and South
America*. Published in two volumes and many editions from 1809
onwards; details for the Canton River are in vol. 2, pp. 362–400 of
the sixth edition, 1852.

8. Hardy, *Register of Ships 1760–1810*, Appendix, pp. 66–72.

9. Ibid., Appendix, p. 75. The pay-book for the *Arniston* shows that
William Blakely received £24 18s 4d for about nine months' service;
BL, IOR/L/MAR/B/149-O(2).

10. Hardy, *Register of Ships 1760–1810*, Appendix, pp. 112–3.

11. BL, IOR/L/MAR/C/850B, ff. 261–2. This is a letter which
Captain W.R. Blakely wrote on 21 February 1835 to J.C. Melville,
secretary to the Court of Directors of EIC, concerning his
pension.

12. The letter of marque is dated 12 November 1812. TNA, ADM
7/319.

13. The ships were joined by two EIC surveying ships, the *Discovery*
and the *Investigator*, which surveyed the area of the Gulf of Pe-
tche-lee after the embassy party had landed. See Horsburgh,
India Directory (1852), vol. 2, pp. 474–8.

14. Henry Ellis, *Journal of the Proceedings of the Late Embassy to China*
(London, 1818); Clarke Abel, *Narrative of a Journey in the Interior of
China* (London, 1818); John M'Leod, *Narrative of a Voyage in His
Majesty's late Ship Alceste to the Yellow Sea* (London, 1817).

15. 43 Geo. III, Cap. 63. Quoted in Hardy, *Register of Ships 1760–
1810*, Appendix, p. 41.

16. In 1821 the fleets to China and India left England between April
and early July. *List of Marine Records of the late East India Company,*

and of subsequent date, preserved in the Record Department of the India Office, London (1896), p. 112.

17. The log of the *Scaleby Castle* for this voyage is at BL, IOR/L/ MAR/B/34N. A chart reproduced in Richard Dunn & Rebekah Higgitt, *Ships, Clocks & Stars, The Quest for Longitude* (London, 2014, paperback edition), pp. 218–9, shows that the latter part of the course taken on this voyage was not often used by ships sailing to China.

18. 'Chart of the China Sea, including the Philippine, Mollucca and Banda Islands, Shewing at the same time all the Tracks into the Pacific Ocean commonly known by the name of the Eastern Passage to China' (George Robertson, 17 November 1790). The chart shows Cloates Island and two positions for the Tryal Rocks. A copy of the chart is at BL, Maps 62710.(2.).

19. *Morning Chronicle*, 8 October 1822. The report came by a ship from St Helena which had anchored there with the *Scaleby Castle* on her return voyage to England.

20. Horsburgh, *India Directory* (1852), vol. 2, p. 638.

21. 'The Honble. Company's Ship Scaleby Castle's track through the Gillolo Passage with the positions of the adjacent Islands & Headlands by Mr. W.R. Blakely. Chief Officer.' A copy of the chart is at BL, Maps 147.e.18.(77.).

22. *Scaleby Castle* log (op. cit.); H. M. Chichester, 'Coffin, John Pine (1778–1830)', rev. Roger T. Stearn, in *DNB* [accessed 23 December 2015]; *Morning Chronicle*, 15 October 1822.

23. The logs of the *Scaleby Castle* and the *Waterloo* for this season are at BL, IOR/L/MAR/B/34S and IOR/L/MAR/B/39H.

24. The dispute is covered in detail in Morse, *Chronicles of the East India Company Trading to China*, vol. IV, pp. 199–221. There is a summary in John Francis Davis, *The Chinese* (London, 1840), p. 47.

25. The charts are entitled 'A Survey of the Passages Leading to the Lymoon' and 'Plan of the Channel to the Eastward of Fansyack'. A copy of the former chart is at BL, 62660.(17.). Horsburgh's

Chart of the Canton River is at BL, Maps 147.e.18. The presentations to the officers are recorded in EIC Court Minutes, BL, IOR/B/183, p. 193, 21 December 1830.

26. Anthony Farrington, *Trading Places: The East India Company and Asia 1600–1834* (British Library, 2002), p. 85. Harriett Low (ed. Nan P. Hodges and Arthur W. Hummel), *Lights and Shadows of a Macao Life* (Woodinville, WA, USA, 2002), Part One, pp. 64–101.

27. Kelsey v. Burnett, 10 February 1831, in *The Annual Register of the Year 1831* (London, 1832), pp. 31–3.

28. The *Scaleby Castle* flew the signal of mutiny at the masthead. Christopher Biden, *Naval Discipline. Subordination contrasted with Insubordination* (London, 1830), p. 18. This book contains many details about the problems with the ships of this fleet.

29. Charles Crompton and John Jervis, *Reports of Cases in the Courts of Exchequer, 1 Will. IV* (London 1832), vol. 1, pp. 291–301; *The Times*, 22 September 1830; *Bell's Weekly Messenger*, 3 October 1830.

30. Low, *Lights and Shadows of a Macao Life*, Part One, p. 101: her diary for 6 February 1830.

31. Biden, *Naval Discipline*, p. 1.

32. Plate 7 is reproduced by permission from the copy of the picture, engraved by Edward Duncan, in the National Maritime Museum collection, image PY8462.

33. Full details of all these arrangements are in EIC Court Minutes, BL, IOR/B/183, pp. 30, 96, 100, 673, 696, 704, 722, 742, 764, between 6 October and 1 December 1830. Captain Burnett's defence cost EIC £339 8s 4d. IOR/B/183, p. 453, 16 February 1831.

34. The quotation is from William's letter to his brother Edward, also quoted earlier. Glasspoole was a contributor to the zoological department of the Norfolk and Norwich Museum, and was the president in 1844.

35. The log of the *Waterloo* for this voyage is at BL, IOR/L/MAR/B/39I.

36. The regulations about conducting divine service were laid down in the instructions issued by EIC to captains. *Orders and Instructions given by the Court of Directors ... to the Commanders of Ships* (London, 1819), p. 34, CXXII [sic, for CXXXII], CXXXIII.

37. Affairs of the East India Company, Minutes of evidence 6 July 1830, *Journal of the House of Lords*, vol. 62, 1830, Appendix 1, pp. 1170–1.

38. The log of the *Waterloo* for the final voyage is at BL, IOR/L/MAR/B/39J.

39. Low, *Lights and Shadows of a Macao Life*, Part Two, pp. 643–89.

40. Horsburgh, *India Directory* (1827), vol. 2, p. 129.

41. In case of sickness or other urgent cause, the captain was permitted to deviate from his sailing instructions, provided he held a meeting of his officers and obtained their opinions. *Orders and Instructions given ... to the Commanders of Ships*, pp. 35–6, CXXXVIII, CXXXIX.

42. Edmund Farrer, *Some Old Houses in Suffolk*, vol. 1, Goswold Hall, p. 43.

43. Ibid., vol. 1, Coulsey Wood, pp. 15–26.

44. Read presented a set of 168 of his etchings and the catalogue to the British Museum, where they may be seen in the Department of Prints and Drawings. Chambers Hall gave his set to the Ashmolean Museum in Oxford; they are in the Western Art Print Room.

45. In 1830 there was a Parliamentary inquiry into the affairs of EIC; its wide coverage included the export of camlets, their price and the rejection of many pieces on the grounds of quality. Affairs of the East India Company: Minutes of evidence: 1 July 1830, *Journal of the House of Lords*, vol. 62: 1830, pp. 1164–8.

46. The relevant page is in the Thrandeston registers at SRO, FB124/D2/6.

47. *Hampshire Advertiser*, 12 December 1874.

5

EDWARD BLAKELY,
SILK MERCER OF NORWICH

Edward, the fourth and youngest son of John Rix and Elizabeth
Blakely, was born on 12 August 1796 and baptised three days
later at Thrandeston. As with his brothers, nothing is known
about his early life at Goswold Hall, but in November 1810
he was at school in Great Yarmouth. This was just a few
months after the death of his father, when he wrote a letter to
his younger sisters Mary Elizabeth and Jane. From the letter
it can be deduced that he was at Southtown School, a small
day and boarding school run by Mr Thomas Wright. During
the school holidays he continued to live with his mother
and sisters at Knapton, but by the time they moved to North
Walsham he would have been old enough to start earning a
living. In contrast to his older brothers John and William, who
travelled abroad at an early age, Edward spent his life in East
Anglia working in the textile trade, becoming in due course a
much-respected member of the community.

Norwich had long been a major centre of the textile
industry in England. In 1335 Queen Philippa, wife of Edward
III, established a colony for the manufacture of cloth in
Norwich, giving employment both to Norfolk workers and
to weavers who were encouraged to come to England from
Flanders. It is recorded that the King and Queen visited
Norwich on three occasions between 1340 and 1344, staying
at the country seat of the prior of the monastery at Trowse

Newton Hall, just outside the city. But the Queen also visited the city at other times, when she was accommodated in the monastic precincts. The gratitude of the people of Norwich to their benefactress resulted in the place where she stayed becoming known as Queen Philippa's house.[1]

Towards the end of the eighteenth century the industry was in a period of decline, but the Norwich manufacturers began to specialise in goods of high quality and the first half of the nineteenth century saw many innovations in what reverted to a flourishing trade. Only the shawl manufacturers at Paisley and Edinburgh in Scotland were able to compete with those in Norwich. In particular there was great demand for women's shawls, which the Norwich firms were able to supply in a quality higher than those from other centres in England. In the 1820s, for example, they produced a very light silk and worsted fabric called challis.[2] Edward moved to Norwich, and he would have spent some time there as an apprentice to one of the many manufacturers or retailers of textiles in the city. On 8 April 1820, when he was only in his early twenties, he opened for business in "the shop at present occupied by Miss [Sarah] Theobald" at 15 Cockey Lane, selling "linen drapery, mercery, &c".[3]

THE THEOBALD FAMILY

The Theobalds were to play a large part in Edward's life in Norwich. Sarah Theobald's father, John Theobald, was born in Norwich in 1736; he was a member of St Mary's Baptist Church and with his first wife Mary, née Masters, he had seven children born between about 1765 and 1777. By trade he was a glover and breeches maker, living in White Lion Lane in the city,[4] and several of his children followed him in the same or similar businesses. His wife died in 1780 and four years later he married

Elizabeth Holmes, a widow from Yarmouth. John died in 1799 and Elizabeth died less than a year later. A memorial to him and to both his wives was erected in St Mary's Church.[5]

John Theobald's eldest son, born about 1765, was also called John. In 1791 he married a widow some eight years his senior, whose maiden name was Mary Steward. Her first marriage, which had lasted just over two years, had been to the Revd Charles Crowe, who was ten years older than her. From 1773 until his death in 1784 Charles had been minister of the independent church at Bradfield. It will be remembered that this was the church near North Walsham to which Edward Blakely's brother John had been directed by Joseph Kinghorn. It is not known how John Theobald the younger came to be in the north of Norfolk, but he married Mary Crowe at North Walsham parish church in 1791; the church register shows that the two witnesses were John and Sarah Steward, Mary's brother and his wife.[6]

Although the church at Bradfield was organised differently from the Particular Baptist congregation in which John had been brought up, the two denominations shared a common Calvinistic theology and sometimes the pastors of one were welcome in the other, as would be shown by the close friendship between John Rix Blakely and the Revd James Browne. One point of difference between the churches was their theology of baptism: whereas the Baptist churches practised believers' baptism for those who were of an age to make their own confession of faith, the church at Bradfield baptised children as infants. John and Mary Theobald had four children who were baptised at Bradfield soon after birth, with their parents being described as "of the Parish of North Walsham". The youngest child was born in 1797 and it was probably after the death of John's father in 1799 that the family moved to Norwich, for in 1802 John Theobald was in business as a breeches maker at 21 Cockey Lane.[7]

The Theobalds were in business in Norwich from the

beginning of the nineteenth century, but when the Blakelys moved from Thrandeston to the North Walsham area in 1810 the Theobald family may still have been remembered there. It is possible that it was through the attendance of Edward's brother John at the church at Bradfield, thereby establishing a link with the Theobalds, that Edward was able to obtain employment in the textile industry in Norwich, or else John may have met the Theobald family during his time in Norwich.

On their move to Norwich at the start of the century John Theobald and his family attended the Old Meeting House, the Nonconformist church in Colegate which John Rix Blakely visited in 1811 and where John Theobald was later a deacon. Whatever the exact circumstances were, it is certain that the Theobald family helped Edward not only to set up in business but also to become part of their family. For on 13 July 1820, three months after his shop opened, Edward married John and Mary Theobald's youngest daughter Elizabeth at the parish church of St Peter Mancroft. The witnesses were Elizabeth's father, her sister-in-law Ruth and Edward's sister Mary Elizabeth.[8]

EDWARD'S RETAIL BUSINESS

John Theobald senior's daughter Sarah and her sister Ann had a retail millinery shop in St George's Bridge Street.[9] Ann withdrew from the business in 1802 on her marriage to Jeremiah Colman, who would become the founder of the Colman's Mustard firm. But Sarah continued to run the business and it was in her shop, which had moved to Cockey Lane in 1812, that Edward began his own career in 1820. For a time Sarah retained the first floor of the premises, where she continued to sell bonnets and other goods and was also engaged in dress-making.

Cockey Lane was a narrow street dating from medieval times and number 15 was on the north side between Little Cockey Lane and Swan Lane. Chase's *Norwich Directory* of 1783 described the street as being

> ... so narrow and irregular, that frequent interruptions, and sometimes accidents, happen by carriages meeting. Persons on foot must squeeze themselves into a dark alley, or burst into a shop, to avoid being run over or crushed against the walls; whilst, in wet weather, you are drenched by torrents of water from the houses, or plunged into a gutter, knee deep.[10]

It would not be until 1856 that the lane was widened, and then to only fifteen feet.[11] It was in one of several areas of the city of Norwich in which there were a number of establishments of the textile trade. Many of these were quite specialised: the descriptions include bombazine dressers, bombazine and crape manufacturers, glovers and breeches makers, haberdashers and hosiers, hatters and hosiers, linen drapers, linen and woollen drapers, milliners and silk mercers. These were retail shops, with much of the actual manufacturing of the goods being done in the workers' homes. Even in the middle of the nineteenth century working conditions were still very poor:

> The factory system is not much in operation, as the work is principally carried on at the houses of the weavers. ... The houses inhabited by the weavers are but little conducive to health or cleanliness, and seem to have been erected without regard to the comfort of the inmates, as the rooms are few in number, and small in dimensions, and are situated in those parts of the city which are unaffected by modern improvements, in sewers or drainage.[12]

Nevertheless, clothes of very high quality were produced, some of which are still in existence in private and public collections.

Edward's business began to prosper within a short time of its opening. As early as September 1820 his advertisement in the *Norfolk Chronicle* described him as a linen draper and silk mercer, and stated that he had just returned from London, where he had selected an extensive collection of silks, satins, shawls and many other articles suitable for the autumn season. In November he advertised for an apprentice and in May 1821 he announced that he furnished funerals, meaning that he was able to supply the mourning clothes which had to be worn on those occasions. He also specialised in the shawls for which Norwich was beginning to be renowned. For example:

> In consequence of the unusual demand for Norwich Shawls and Scarfs, E. B. has provided for the present season a more elegant and valuable Selection than he has hitherto held.
>
> Advertisement in *Norfolk Chronicle*, 12 May 1821.

EDWARD'S FAMILY

Later in the same year Cockey Lane was renamed London Lane, but the numbers of the houses and shops were unaltered and number 15 served both as Edward's retail premises and also as a home for himself and his wife. In 1824 Elizabeth gave birth to their daughter but there must have been serious problems, for the baby died on 28 April and on 14 May Elizabeth also died. This was some years before the compulsory registration of births, marriages and deaths, but Edward had joined the Theobald family in attending the Old Meeting House and the church burial register for that period is available.[13] It records the death and burial of Elizabeth but there is no entry for her daughter, suggesting that the child died at or soon after birth. The only evidence for the nameless baby's short life is on a memorial tablet to Elizabeth, which Edward placed in the church and which is still there.

But Edward's sadness at losing his wife and daughter was fairly brief, for on 21 December of the following year he married again. His second wife was also called Elizabeth Theobald; she was cousin to his first wife, being the eldest daughter of Thomas Theobald and his wife Elizabeth. Thomas was the youngest son of John Theobald senior: in 1801 he had married Elizabeth Colman, sister of Jeremiah, who has already been mentioned. The families of Theobald and Colman were closely linked, and a further link would come later when Elizabeth (née Colman)'s granddaughter married Jeremiah James Colman, who took over the running of the Colman firm in 1854 on the death of his father. Edward's new father-in-law Thomas was also in business in Norwich, as a partner in the firm of Booth, Theobald and Booth, who were manufacturers of bombazine and crape. He was very wealthy and his private account book shows that he gave Elizabeth a present of £2,000 on her marriage, which would be worth about £150,000 at present-day values. He gave the same sum to his daughter Sarah on her marriage to William Hardy Cozens in 1830.[14]

Edward and Elizabeth's first child was born in December 1826, a son who was named Edward Theobald Blakely. He was followed by two daughters, Ellen Mary in 1829 and Eliza in 1831. Edward's family tree is shown in Figure 4. Birth records from Nonconformist churches in this period had to be registered at Dr Williams's Library in London in 1837, and the births of the three children were thus registered in February of that year, with the signatures of Edward, Elizabeth and Elizabeth's mother, together with that of the eminent Norwich surgeon William Dalrymple.[15]

The family of Edward Blakely

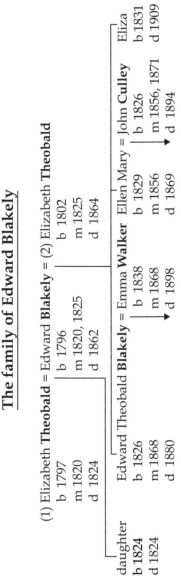

Figure 4

It was not, however, a particularly happy time for Elizabeth. Her parents were members of St Mary's Baptist Church in Norwich, where some of the church members formed business associations. One of these was a partnership in two concerns between Thomas Theobald, John Darken and Samuel Colman, the last being Elizabeth Theobald's brother. The businesses were an iron foundry in Norwich and a water mill at Ware Park in Hertfordshire, in both of which Thomas Theobald lost an enormous amount of money and he was eventually made bankrupt. His private ledger provides detailed accounts of his wealth during the whole of his business life. From 1821 until 1825 his net assets exceeded £25,000, but he lost everything owing to the activities of his partners, "two hardened Knaves, ... Villains [who] deceived and robbed [him]".[16] The dispute between Thomas Theobald and John Darken was investigated by a committee of St Mary's Church, with the result that in 1830 Thomas and his wife had to withdraw from membership.[17] To combine business and religious activities in this way might seem unusual to modern readers, but Nonconformist churches in nineteenth-century Norwich did exert a considerable influence on the commercial life of the city – usually, it must be said, for the benefit of the population.

SILK MERCER TO THE QUEEN

The period from about 1825 until 1852 was Edward's most successful time as a retailer of high quality goods. In 1826, 1832 and 1840 he enlarged his shop; a description of the extended premises as they were in 1850 will be given later. On several occasions he took on assistants; in 1841 he wanted "a young man ... who is willing to conform to the rules adopted in a Dissenting Family".[18] Perhaps this was one of the three young men who, with two young women, were living with Edward's family above the shop in the census of that year. Edward's customers were the ladies of Norwich and the surrounding area; later on he would advertise particularly to the nobility and gentry.

Between 1826 and 1830 there were several riots in Norwich involving the weavers, due in part to the increased use of machinery in the manufacturing processes. Machines were introduced to enable the Norwich trade to compete better with the textile manufacturers in the north of England, but specialised merchants such as Edward continued to sell goods produced in a more traditional manner. In 1829 he advertised that any lady who bought a dress made from merino wool, which he had purchased, would receive a ticket to enable a good unemployed weaver to find work. This was, perhaps, his earliest scheme for aiding those in Norwich who were disadvantaged in some way; it was an example of his developing social conscience. Two years later, when the textile industry in Norwich was still at a low ebb, a report in the *Huntingdon, Bedford & Peterborough Gazette* paid tribute to this fabric called Norwich Saxon Merino which was made by Messrs Bolingbroke and was on sale at Mr Blakely's and elsewhere, and the report expressed the hope that the use of this material would do much to restore the fortunes of the industry and its workers.[19]

It was not long before the firms which made and sold dresses, shawls and other finery for the ladies of society began to receive commands to send specimens to the royal court. William Keppel, the fourth Earl of Albemarle, and his second wife Charlotte, who lived in Norfolk, were the intermediaries between the Norwich businesses and the court of Queen Adelaide. The Queen had expressed a wish for her ladies to wear dresses and shawls which were made in Britain, and the Countess of Albemarle approached Messrs Willett about the design of an appropriate dress and Edward Blakely's business for the supply of shawls.

Soon these firms received orders from the Queen to send her the dress and some specimens of Norwich shawls. From the shawls which were sent, three were selected which were made by Messrs Shickle of Elm Hill.[20] Making the most of the opportunity, Edward placed an advertisement in the press inviting the ladies of Norwich to inspect a selection of the same shawls which had been sent to the Queen, who was patronising their manufacture. In the next month, April 1831, and as a direct result of his sending these shawls to Queen Adelaide, Edward was appointed a Silk Mercer and Furrier to the Queen.[21] This was a prestigious honour, and one which he was pleased to hold for many years.

The coronation of King William IV and his Queen took place in September and celebrations were held in Norwich as in many other places; it was reported that the city was splendidly decorated and special mention was made of the illuminations on Mr Blakely's house. In the following years Edward marked the birthday of the Queen by decorating his premises lavishly, with lamps in the form of a crown and star and spelling out slogans such as "Adelaide, the patroness of Norwich Manufactures".

The Queen's opposition to political change made her unpopular at the time leading up to the Reform Act of 1832 and Edward thought it wise to take down, for a short while, the royal coat of arms which was above his shop. At the same time the landlord of the Queen Adelaide Inn took out his paintbrush and obliterated the Queen's head on his signboard. But before long calm returned to the streets and Edward made sure that he kept on good terms with his patroness by sending her shawls and other garments, particularly at the time of her birthday. The first of these gifts to the royal household was made in January 1833 when, with the assistance of the Earl of Albermarle, he sent a particularly fine cloak which had been made by Messrs Shickle and Towler. The cloak was described in intricate detail in a newspaper report and a letter of thanks was sent to Edward by the Queen's Treasurer expressing her appreciation of receiving "so handsome a specimen of Norwich manufacture".[22]

To judge by his regular advertisements in the newspapers, Edward's stock was large and varied. He adapted what he had for sale to suit the times of the year, also selling off surplus stock at the end of the season. Norwich shawls were perhaps his most expensive articles, but his other wares included cloaks, silk dresses, chintzes, satins and lace, and in 1837 he announced that he was entering into the linen trade and would stock linen for the table and for babies.

In the same year King William IV died and was succeeded by the young Queen Victoria, to whom Edward sent a mourning shawl, which was reported to be the most costly ever made in England.[23] Over the next few years the range of goods which he sold increased, and in March 1840 he announced that he proposed to make considerable alterations to his establishment and would sell off his existing stock at reduced prices. Two months later he was still trying to dispose of his winter goods but had paid a visit to London, where he had selected a wide variety of fashionable articles for the spring and summer. Another journey to buy merchandise in London followed in November, but in the following two or three years he began to concentrate more on fabrics made in Norwich and especially on shawls.

There are several indications at this time and later of his aspirations and rising prosperity. In April 1842 he advertised under the heading of "Queen's Shawls" that he had a "splendid assortment" of Norwich shawls which both the Queen (Victoria) and the Queen Dowager (Adelaide) had been pleased to patronise.[24] The advertisement also drew attention to improvements which had recently taken place in the manufacture of shawls, with the result that the skill of the artisans meant that shawls were being made of almost the same quality as those from India. In the early 1840s Norwich textile manufacturing was going through another period of depression, and it is clear that Edward was aiming to obtain and sell goods of the highest quality which he hoped that ladies of wealth would be anxious to buy when they learnt that royalty and the nobility were also buying them.

To this end Edward managed to secure the patronage of an impressive list of people, many of whom were titled ladies. In 1842 the list began with the two British queens, followed by the Queen of the Belgians, five duchesses and four other named ladies, together with unnamed members of the nobility and the gentry. By 1849 there were, in addition to the three queens, eight duchesses, twelve marchionesses, countesses and viscountesses, many ladies and several with the plain title Miss or Mrs, together with a few gentlemen, in a list of seventy-five people. It is perhaps doubtful whether these patrons actually bought many of Edward's shawls and other garments, but his hope was that other people would do so and his business seems to have been flourishing.

THE FAMILY HOME, COAT OF ARMS AND HOLIDAYS

Edward's children were now growing up and the family needed more room than the cramped accommodation above the shop could provide. In 1842 or 1843 they moved out of the centre of Norwich to a substantial house called The Mount in the village of Thorpe Hamlet, less than a mile to the east of the city. The house was not new: in a sale advertisement of 1810, when it was called Thorpe Mount, it had two small parlours and two bedrooms above, with a small garden, but Edward or a previous occupier had it enlarged. When the Blakely family lived there it had a large drawing room, a dining room and a library downstairs, with two large bedrooms and other rooms upstairs; Pevsner described it as being of yellow brick with a Greek Doric porch.[25] The grounds, of about a third of an acre in extent, were entered through iron gates in a stone wall. Befitting its name, the house stood on rising ground with views towards the River Wensum, Norwich Castle and the cathedral.[26] The house is no longer in existence, having been demolished in 1972 when the area was redeveloped, although its stone boundary wall still marks its position.

Since becoming Silk Mercer and Furrier to the Queen in 1831, Edward had displayed the royal coat of arms on his billheads and above the door of his shop, but he decided that he would like to have his own coat of arms as well. He approached the Heralds' College (as the College of Arms was then known) to grant him arms – partly, no doubt, to boost his business, but also as a sign of his rising social status at a time when such things mattered more than they do today. He knew about his Rix and Grey ancestry and that both these families had had coats of arms, and the Heralds were evidently satisfied that arms based on those held by his ancestors could be granted to him. The grant was made on 30 May 1843 and the description in the letters patent reads:

> Quarterly First and Fourth Argent a Lion rampant Gules semé of Trefoils Or within a bordure dovetail of the second for BLAKELY, Second and Third Azure a Fesse between two Unicorns' heads erased in chief and a Cross patée in base Or for RIX And for the Crest On a Wreath of the Colours An Unicorn passant Azure Gutte d'Or and ducally gorged Argent resting

the dexter leg upon a Escocheon Or charged with a pale Vair.[27]

The lion rampant in the first and fourth quarters is the lion of the arms of the Greys of Thrandeston, and thus the Blakely family was clearly linked with their ancestors who had lived at Goswold Hall since the late fifteenth century. The motto is '*Allons Dieu Ayde*', which can be translated as 'Let us go on, with God as our help'. The arms are shown as the frontispiece to this book.

Despite his business taking up a good deal of his time, Edward was able to take the opportunity of leaving Norwich for holidays. As early as the summer of 1828 he took his family to the seaside, probably Yarmouth, and they were certainly there in 1833. When his son Edward Theobald (who will now be referred to as 'Edward T') was older he took him on trips to see various places in England and Wales in the summers of 1841, 1842 and 1843, and in 1844 Edward T went to Germany and Switzerland in the company of a gentleman whom his father may have engaged for the purpose.

These trips seem to have been partly for educational purposes, for Edward T kept detailed notes, which he wrote into a travel diary. This document is in the archives of the Norfolk Record Office and it gives a fascinating account of where they went and what they saw.[28] The first and third of the journeys are written up fully and illustrated with postcards, whereas the other two are in the form of notes. On the first journey in August 1841 Edward T and his parents were accompanied by Elizabeth's sister, Sarah, and her husband William Hardy Cozens.[29] They travelled by stagecoach from Norwich and then by coaches, hired carriages and steam trains across the Midlands and on to Liverpool. From there they travelled to North Wales, where the highlight was an ascent of Snowdon by the "Pony track" route; the men walked but the ladies rode on ponies. The weather was fine, which was fortunate, as they did not start until early afternoon. However, they were rewarded with good views from the top and returned safely, all using ponies for part of the descent.

They then journeyed through the Welsh Marches to Hereford and Monmouth, after which they visited Bath to see Edward's brother Thomas and his family. Thomas had been living in Bath since 1823, where he earned his living as a haberdasher, though perhaps not with the same success as his brother in Norwich. The journey back to London was by train: Brunel's broad gauge line from Bristol and Bath to Paddington had been opened less than two months earlier. From London they travelled back to Norwich by coach. As well as telling the reader what they did, Edward T included a good deal of the history of the places they visited. They travelled, according to the diary, a distance of 920 miles and were away from home for two weeks.

In 1842 Edward took his son to London for a week, also visiting Windsor and Hampton Court. In the following year father and son spent ten days on a tour which included Winchester, the Isle of Wight and the New Forest. As they passed through London on the outward journey, Edward had some business to conduct which included a visit to the Heralds' College; his grant of arms had been made three months earlier, and doubtless there were some papers to collect or a bill to pay. While staying in Ryde on the Isle of Wight they had a close view of the Queen and Prince Albert, who were just arriving on the island. Again, Edward T recounted some of the history of the places they saw, notably Winchester Cathedral and Carisbrooke Castle. His writing style is good and the inclusion of several literary quotations indicates that, at the age of sixteen, he was quite well educated.

THE JENNY LIND CONCERTS AND
FURTHER EXPANSION

Edward had an increasing awareness of the need for improvements in the welfare of the inhabitants of Norwich, for which he was able to use his prospering business. He was involved when, in January 1849, the celebrated Swedish singer Jenny Lind gave two concerts in Norwich, the purpose of which was to raise money for charity. Most generously, Miss Lind did not make any charge for her performances.

On her arrival in Norwich she was welcomed by the bishop, the mayor and other dignitaries, and on their behalf Edward Blakely presented her with a fillover white shawl and dress, together with a green llama printed scarf from his own business.[30] The concerts, given in St Andrew's Hall, were very popular, with more than 4,000 tickets being sold. Half of them were for the most expensive seats, costing half a guinea. Among the audience was Jeremiah James Colman, then a young man of eighteen, who was "exceedingly pleased with [Jenny Lind], no less for the charming simplicity of her manners, than for her singing".[31] The total amount raised was £1,253, a considerable sum for that time, and the proceeds were used to found a hospital for children in Norwich. This was opened in 1854 and it is still in existence today as the Jenny Lind Children's Hospital, part of the Norfolk and Norwich University Hospital. On the day following Miss Lind's second concert Edward entertained her, the bishop and his family, the mayor and about a dozen other people to luncheon at his house in Thorpe Hamlet. It is clear that Edward was becoming well known and respected in Norwich as a responsible retailer of goods manufactured there, and as one who was concerned about the interests of the workers.

The years 1849 and 1850 were ones in which Edward's success enabled him to expand his business and to extend his reputation in several ways, both in Norwich and in London. Early in 1849 he was awarded a silver medal for his shawl fabrics by the Society of Arts in London.[32] In addition to showing examples of his shawls, he displayed some lace collars which had been made by children in a school run by the bishop's daughter, Mary Stanley. These were poor children to whom Miss Stanley was able to give something of worth that they could do, while at the same time giving them "careful tuition in the duties of morality", as a later newspaper report put it.[33]

Bishop Stanley was well known for his philanthropic activities and his daughter followed his lead, later becoming a nurse in the Crimean War. One of the members of the committee who judged the prizes at the exhibition was Sir John Boileau, a prominent member of society in Norfolk and London, who owned the Ketteringham estate near Norwich. In March Sir John wrote a letter to Edward congratulating him on his award, and expressing the hope that it would lead to increased sales and to more workers finding employment.[34] It was about this time that Edward opened a shop in London, at 7 Conduit Street, near Regent Street. Sir John's letter refers to this shop, saying that he and his wife could easily call there to look at the shawls which were on sale. Clearly Edward's clientele was widening beyond Norwich to society ladies in the capital.

Edward was also involved with the Norwich School of Design. This had been founded in 1845 and was one of fourteen such schools in the provinces of England and Scotland, together with three in Ireland, which were partly funded by the government. Their purpose was to improve the standards in design in various branches of manufacturing businesses, but it is clear from one of the reports by the inspector from the Board of Trade, Mr Ambrose Poynter, that most Norwich manufacturers preferred to rely on their existing (and experienced) designers, rather than to employ younger designers from the school.[35] This report was based on an inspection carried out in November 1849 but, following a second inspection in May 1850, Mr Poynter wrote that it was "gratifying to state that one of the shawl manufacturers has at length selected a pupil from the school to assist his designer, and that he has made application for another. ... It is the first example which has occurred at Norwich of this mode of connexion between the school and the manufactory."[36] Edward was a member of the committee of the School of Design, and in the autumn of 1849 he had opened a shawl manufactory in Norwich. Although the report does not mention him by name, it is very probable that he was the manufacturer concerned, and this is also the view of the authors of a book about the Norwich School.[37]

Edward's manufactory was by the bridge over the River Wensum at Duke's Palace in the heart of the city's cloth and dyeing industry. He evidently decided that to run a thriving retail business in London Street (as London Lane had been called since 1829) and at the same time to be in charge of a new manufacturing base was too much for him, and he installed his son Edward T as manager of the River House Manufactory and Print Works, as it became known. After just a few months the local press was enthusiastically commending the project, as the firm of Messrs Blakely was now manufacturing goods of very high quality as well as selling them. Furthermore, it gave employment to fillover weavers who, a few years earlier, had been forced to leave Norwich for Paisley and other textile centres.

From this time Edward's advertisements included the addresses of all three of his premises: in London Street and Duke's Palace in Norwich, and in Conduit Street in London. By the spring of 1850 his retail shop occupied both 15 and 16 London Street. It is not clear whether this was a further expansion or simply a renumbering, but the building was both extensive and imposing. It included a ground-floor shop with showrooms on the first floor and ample living accommodation above, for which there was a

Edward Blakely advertisement in
David Copperfield, June 1850
Image © The British Library Board (Mic. B.613/75)
Plate 8

separate doorway from the street, the whole stretching back from
the narrow street a distance of eighty-four feet.[38] Considerable
rebuilding in the centre of Norwich in the early 1970s resulted in
the demolition of this part of the street, but a late nineteenth-century
print and an early twentieth-century photograph show glimpses of
part of the building. The best indication of the grandeur is seen in
one of Edward's advertisements, which included a drawing of the
front of the premises: this was a half-page insertion in one of the
monthly parts of Charles Dickens's *David Copperfield* and is shown
in Plate 8.[39]

SHERIFF OF NORWICH

At a personal level, and also in his business, Edward's most
successful years were 1850 and 1851. His contacts with some
of the establishment figures have already been mentioned, and
his reputation in the city of Norwich had steadily increased.
His business was in the retail and manufacturing trades, and he
had done a good deal to enhance the reputation of the city and
to secure employment for the industrious and capable working
population. In addition he had devoted time and energy to the
needs of those who were often neglected in Victorian society.
The city had both a mayor and a sheriff, each of whom served
for a year, the latter sometimes becoming mayor, and it was
in November 1850 that Edward took up his post as sheriff.
This was an honour which was paid to him in gratitude for
all the work which he had done, but it was accompanied by
many formal duties and doubtless substantial expenses which,
unlike some of today's civic figures, he would not have been
able to reclaim.

The mayor during Edward's year of office was Henry
Woodcock who, unusually, was serving for the second year
in succession. Mr Woodcock was not a young man and he
suffered from ill health, so Edward had to perform some
duties which the mayor would normally have done. But, to

judge by the press reports at the end of his time as sheriff, Edward was very successful in his civic role. It was said that "his official position enabled him to bring its manufactures more prominently forward than could have been done by a private individual". His general duties were carried out with dignity and "his hospitable entertainments [were] extended to the poor and needy".[40]

In July 1851 he was among the group of dignitaries who met Prince Albert, the husband of Queen Victoria, on his arrival at Ipswich railway station to attend a meeting of the British Association.[41] But Edward was also to be found organising events for ordinary members of the public. Later in the same month he played a leading role in arranging for 350 Norwich textile workers to go to London in order to visit the Great Exhibition in Hyde Park. This was not a day trip, as it would be today, but one where overnight accommodation had to be provided. The Member of Parliament for Norwich, Morton Peto, was also involved and he entertained the whole party to a sumptuous dinner, at which Edward gave a lengthy speech.[42]

Another visit which Edward helped to organise was a visit of more than 200 parishioners from Hitcham, near Stowmarket, to Norwich, to have a tour of the textile factories and some of the public buildings of the city. Towards the end of his time in office he was present at the opening of the Norwich Water Works. This gave the inhabitants of the city a proper supply of water, which helped to reduce disease, including cholera which was prevalent at this time in many parts of the country. Once again Edward gave a speech, which was printed verbatim in the local press reports of the occasion.

Reports are also to be found of some of the dinners which Edward attended as sheriff. In August he gave the Sheriff's Dinner at the Royal Hotel in Norwich, which was attended by nearly a hundred gentlemen including the mayor, the Member of Parliament and many others involved in city affairs, together with some from London. Many toasts were drunk and speeches made and if Edward had to pay the whole bill himself, as is likely, it must have cost him a large amount of money. Unlike some of the other city dignitaries, his income was derived almost entirely from his business, but he must have been aware of the financial implications of his office before he agreed to be appointed as sheriff. However, he was, from all reports, a very successful sheriff and at the end of his time he was entertained to dinner by the legal establishment of Norwich in return for the hospitality that they had received from him, and also as a mark of respect for the way in which he had served the city during the year.

THE GREAT EXHIBITION

Although Edward's duties as sheriff must have occupied a considerable amount of time, his main preoccupation during the year was with his business. For 1851 was the year of the Great Exhibition, and he was anxious to make the most of the undoubtedly fine shawls and other goods which ladies bought from him. It may have been the impending Exhibition that led him to start up as a manufacturer as well as being a retailer and also to open his shop in London. The Exhibition was held in the Crystal Palace, built for the purpose in Hyde Park, and brought together examples from all branches of industry in Britain together with many exhibits from abroad, for its full title was 'The Great Exhibition of the Works of Industry of all Nations'. Edward's expressed intention was to exhibit some of the shawls that his business had made, in particular what were described as Anglo-Indian shawls, which he claimed were as fine as those which came from India itself. Particular mention was also made in the long newspaper reports of Messrs Blakely's fillover shawls, which successfully rivalled many of the similar goods from France.

Most of the Norwich manufacturers of high-class ladies' apparel also showed their wares at the Exhibition, including Messrs Towler, Campin & Co. of Elm Hill, Messrs Bolingbroke of St Clement's, Messrs Willett of Pottergate Street and Messrs Clabburn and Plummer of Pitt Street. Prior to the goods being sent to London, the firms displayed the finery in their premises to the ladies of Norwich. At the Crystal Palace "the valuable and interesting display of British shawls has been most judiciously arranged in the gallery on the south-western side of the transept, the London and Norwich contributions being placed in a series of elegantly-designed glass cases".[43] The Exhibition was open from 1 May to 15 October 1851, and more than six million visits were made to see it, although that number includes repeat visits by many people, particularly those who lived in or near London.

The concept of the Great Exhibition had been announced at the meeting of the Society of Arts in 1849 at which Edward had been presented with his silver medal by the president, Prince Albert.[44] The Prince was, to a large extent, the originator of the Exhibition and both he and the Queen paid very many visits to the Crystal Palace. The highlight, as far as the Blakelys were concerned, was the two-hour visit that the royal couple made on the morning of Saturday 14 June. In her journal the Queen wrote about her visits to the Exhibition, and the entry for this day included an account of her inspection of the shawls which were on show:

> Went 1[rst] through one or two of the French Courts, & then upstairs, to examine in detail the Norwich shawls, of the lightest Cashmir material, also of silk, with beautiful designs, & very light Grenadine printed shawls, made in the neighbourhood of London.[45]

The Norwich shawl manufacturers were represented by at least eight firms and it was reported that:

Her Majesty stayed sometime at the case which contains the goods exhibited by Messrs. Blakely, of Norwich, and was graciously pleased to express her approval of a purple silk centre shawl, the pattern of which was designed expressly for the Exhibition. ... Her Majesty was also graciously pleased to grant permission to Mr. Blakely to display his blue and gold, and green and gold long shawls in imitation of the Delhi Cashmeres, being composed of real Cashmere wool with the Indian pine in gold; these are deserving of particular attention, as being of a different manufacture from any other British shawls in the Exhibition. ... Her Majesty was graciously pleased to give an order to Mr. Blakely for the blue and gold Cashmere long shawl.[46]

As the manager of the manufacturing side of the family's business, Edward T was on duty at the stand when the royal party arrived, and it was to him that the Queen gave her order. The firm had been the recipient of many congratulatory articles in the East Anglian press, but to have the Queen buy a shawl from their stock was an enormous boost to their reputation. The shawl was illustrated in *The Art Journal Illustrated Catalogue* of the Exhibition, which described it in glowing terms: "in its simple yet elegant design, and in tasteful arrangement of colour, it is everything to be desired." [47]

When the party had left, Edward T was so overjoyed that he sent a message to his father, who was looking after the business in Norwich, to tell him the good news. The Electric Telegraph Company had set up its main office at the Exhibition at the south entrance, and telegraphic messages could be sent from there to many of the main towns in England, Wales and Scotland. Edward T wrote that "The Queen has purchased of us", but in his excitement he made a mistake in the address. He directed the message to 7 Conduit Street, Norwich, mixing up the London

BLAKELY'S SHAWLS,

Patronized by her Majesty the QUEEN.

EDWARD BLAKELY

INVITES the attention of the Ladies to his present Stock of

ANGLO-INDIAN SHAWLS

AND

NORWICH POPLINS,

Which have recently been honoured by the distinguished Patronage of Royalty.

15 and 16, London-street,
7, Conduit-street, Regent-street, London.

MANUFACTORY,

THE RIVER HOUSE, NORWICH.

Edward Blakely advertisement in
the Norfolk Chronicle, 6 September 1851
Image © The British Library. All Rights Reserved
Plate 9

shop with the Norwich one, but it nevertheless arrived at 15 London Street in Norwich. In 1851 the telegraph was a new and expensive method of communication: this short message would have cost about 6s 8d, equivalent to £37 at today's prices.

The Queen was pleased with her new shawl and in July Edward was delighted to receive another order from her, this time for a white Cashmere shawl resembling one of those she had seen in the Exhibition.[48] Edward made the most of his royal sales by placing appropriate advertisements in the Norwich papers: Plate 9 shows an advertisement which he placed in the Norfolk Chronicle in September.[49] At the close of the Exhibition in October specially constituted juries made the awards: a prize medal was awarded in Class XV to Edward Theobald Blakely for his 'Collection of Shawls and also Barège scarfs of a novel taste'.[50]

Edward's period of office as sheriff came to an end in November, and he was then able to give full attention to his business. In the spring of the following year he offered, for eight guineas each, Norwich shawls in the design for which he had been awarded a prize medal at the Great Exhibition. In February there was a short article about the manufacturing and design aspects of his business in a prestigious fashion magazine, in which the readers' attention was drawn to his London premises.[51] A few months later three Blakely shawls, including copies of the two bought by the Queen, were loaned for display at lectures given at the Society of Arts in London, a gesture much appreciated by those who were present.[52] Edward was evidently trying to make his merchandise known among the ladies of society in the capital.

BANKRUPTCY AND HIS CLOSING YEARS

At the same time Edward began to import robed prints and muslins from the printworks of Blech, Steinbach and Mantz of Mulhouse in France, near the border with Switzerland. This was a well-known and respectable company which had also exhibited at the Great Exhibition, but Edward's sale of their goods represented a departure from his Norwich shawls and it soon became clear that all was not well. He was selling off at reduced prices the stock which he had left over from the previous season. This was something that he had often done before, but the quantity of material was much greater than in the past.

In the summer of 1852 he advertised that goods of the current season were being sold at lower prices than previously: he had bought a large stock of Austrian shawls and goods from a Paisley manufacturer who had retired, all of which were being sold at half price. In November he opened another shop in Norwich, to be managed by Mr R.G. Holmes, where a wide variety of stock would be sold "on the most advantageous terms for Ready Money". Rather ominously, the first advertisement for this shop had the heading 'BLAKELY'S CHEAP WAREHOUSE'. It appears that he had much more stock than he could sell and, in fact, the new shop had been opened on the recommendation of the manager of the East of England Bank in Norwich as a way of clearing out some of the surplus goods. In January 1853 there was a large sale of shawls and other goods at 7 Conduit Street but, strangely, the advertisement in the *Morning Chronicle* did not state that it was Blakely's shop. In the middle of March he was still advertising that he had "a large number of Woven and Printed Shawls, which will be Sold at unusually low prices" at his three retail establishments in Norwich and London.[53]

This was Edward's last such advertisement, for a few days later his cheques were refused by his bankers and on 9 April 1853 he was declared bankrupt.[54] It is worth remarking that no hint of his financial difficulties found its way into family documents or even family folklore in the twentieth century.

It is clear that those of his generation knew all about them, as did the next generation, but Victorian secrecy meant that, almost certainly, the news travelled no further. With hindsight there is an indication of trouble in the letter which Edward's sister Mary Elizabeth wrote to her nephew in 1872, where she said that "there are many painful remembrances connected with the place [Norwich]", because the problems were not confined to him.

Less than three weeks later, on 28 April, Edward T was also declared bankrupt.[55] The downfall of both father and son seems to have originated with Edward T, manager of the manufacturing side of the business, being considerably overdrawn at his bank as early as 1850. He asked for a further loan of £2,500, which was granted with his father as surety.[56] Furthermore, in 1851 Edward, as an executor of the estate of his late brother William Rix, had transferred £2,500 from that estate to his own account without the knowledge of Mary Elizabeth, who was his co-executor. It is difficult to unravel the exact causes of their bankruptcies from the intricate details of the Bankruptcy Court cases which followed, but among the newspaper reports is one which has a verbatim account of the questioning which Edward underwent and it makes rather sad reading: several times he said that he was unable to recollect the explanation for some of the details in the accounts, even those which he had written himself.[57] His business had become too complex for him to be able to manage properly, especially in the previous two or three years when he was setting up Edward T as a manufacturer in what was intended to be an independent business.

Following the declaration of bankruptcy, the due processes of the law immediately rolled into action. Edward had to sell everything he owned in order to raise the cash to pay off his creditors. Advertisements appeared in the press for the sale of his business premises, his draper's stock and his house and possessions. His post as an alderman of Norwich was terminated. Edward's premises in London Street were bought by another Norwich silk mercer and linen draper, N.H. Caley, whose business remained there for the next seventy years. The stocks of shawls, dresses and other textiles, valued at many thousands of pounds, were bought by a number of different merchants, who sold them on to the public.

The Mount, his house at Thorpe Hamlet, was bought by Thomas Jarrold, head of the Norwich printing and publishing firm. The list of articles for sale from the house included many valuable items: a "remarkably fine old oak cabinet dated 1661", which is likely to have come from Goswold Hall; Chinese tables, a Margetts chronometer and a large quantity of Indian china which had been passed on from his brother, Captain William Rix Blakely; and a set of 168 etchings by David Charles Read. The latter appears to be identical with the set of Read's etchings in two volumes which the artist presented to the British Museum. In addition, all Edward T's equipment at the manufactory was auctioned: the stock included warping mills, looms and Jacquard engines.[58] Mary Elizabeth, who was unmarried, had been living with Edward at The Mount, and she now had to make her home elsewhere. She moved to Bath to live with her other brother Thomas and his wife Charlotte, and spent the rest of her life there.

Several meetings were held at the Court of Bankruptcy in the next few months. In July a first dividend of 7s 6d in the pound was paid to Edward's creditors, and on 9 September a meeting was held to determine the outcome of the cases of both Edward and Edward T.[59] The main points in Edward's favour were that he was very well respected in Norwich, that he had managed a large and profitable business for many years and that he did have unusually large assets, including his properties. These matters impressed Mr Commissioner Fane in his analysis of the case, and he granted both Edward and Edward T first-class certificates which, following the Bankruptcy Consolidation Act of 1849, were given in cases where the bankruptcy of a "virtuous" debtor was attributed to unavoidable losses and misfortune.[60]

Three weeks later, on Saturday 1 October, Edward opened for business again in a substantial shop on the north side of Queen Street, not far from his former premises in London Street. The shop had a frontage of forty-five feet and extended back nearly eighty feet, with the retail department on the ground floor and living quarters for himself and his family on the three floors above.[61] In his advertisements Edward announced that he had new stock including silks, shawls, fancy dresses, mantles, furs, linen and lace. His good reputation may have meant that some of his former suppliers were willing to let him have goods in advance of payment in the expectation of a return to profitable trading, but the conditions of his bankruptcy meant that he needed to recommence his business so that eventually it could be wound up, providing further funds for the creditors.[62] He occupied the new premises for about the next four years, selling goods similar to those he sold before his bankruptcy but perhaps of lower quality.

However, it would seem that, despite the apparent success of the business, it was not making any money: Edward had almost certainly lost the custom of those who used to purchase articles of high value, including the nobility and gentry part of his clientele. It was not until May 1857 that a second dividend of 5¾d in the pound was paid, making the total payment to his creditors just less than 8s in the pound.[63] Following one of the provisions of the Bankruptcy Act of 1705, this meant that Edward would receive none of the value of the estate recovered, and on 25 May he signed an indenture which assigned all his stock in trade and all his personal estate and effects to the two official assignees to distribute to his creditors.[64] The once-successful silk mercer of Norwich was ruined.

No longer being able to live in the centre of Norwich, Edward and his wife moved to live in a semi-detached house in West Parade, off Earlham Road on the west side of the city. In order to have something to live on, Edward advertised that he had dresses, cloaks and other goods for sale, that he made gentlemen's shirts to order and that he supplied families with mourning outfits and other necessities for funerals. His last advertisement appeared in December 1860, perhaps because his health was failing. It can be inferred that his bankruptcy affected his state of health as well as his personal finances, for on 24 May 1862 he died of emphysema and heart disease at the age of sixty-five years.

So ended the life of one of the main retailers of ladies' clothing in Norwich, whose business was highly regarded by those in the upper echelons of society in the city, who cared greatly for the working men and women and who, by his family and business relationships, was able to get alongside people in authority, particularly some of the Nonconformists like himself, whose influence in trade and business was substantial.

EDWARD'S ACTIVITIES OUTSIDE HIS BUSINESS

The fact that Edward lost all his possessions when he became bankrupt is one reason why the main line of the Blakely family has almost nothing that belonged to him. Much of what is known about him, which has been recounted in this chapter, has been obtained from official records and contemporary material in newspapers and other publications. As a successful businessman in the first half of the nineteenth century he would have worked long hours, with little time left for leisure. His attendance at Nonconformist chapel services does not seem to have played as large a part in his life as it did for some of his friends, such as the Colman family. But he did have time for one particular pursuit later in his life, and that was local archaeology. Although he may have reasoned that by joining the Norfolk and Norwich Archaeological Society he would come into contact with those in Norwich society whom it would be useful to know, he did make some contributions to the meetings, including showing some "interesting antiquities" at one of the first meetings in 1846. At a later meeting he showed a seventeenth-century purse, and in 1858 he took an early eighteenth-century snuff-box and a seventeenth-century ivory piercer to meetings of the British Archaeological Association.

But from 1848 or earlier he had in his possession a more substantial piece of Norwich history. This was a pair of magistrates' posts which dated from the time of Henry VIII. In earlier times posts such as these were often placed outside the houses of mayors and other officials in Norwich, and in 1848 Edward wrote a paper on his posts for the Norfolk and Norwich Archaeological Society.[65] An article in *Norfolk Archaeology* in 1852 referred to these posts, stating that "a pair of them stood, within the memory of persons now living, at a door near Elm Hill, and are now at the house of E. Blakeley, Esq., at Thorpe".[66] It is thus clear that Edward had the posts at The Mount and, from a later reference, that he took them with him when he moved to Earlham Road.[67] None of the sources gives any indication of how or why Edward obtained possession of the posts: it may be conjectured that he had some aspiration of becoming mayor of Norwich and decided to "rescue" them from possible destruction. The posts were quite substantial, being carved from solid oak and about 7 ft 6 in. high. Illustrations of them had been published in an article in another journal in 1821, and it is this article to which several later writers refer.[68] After Edward's death the posts remained in the Norwich area, possibly with the

Colman family; in 1931 they were bought for the city and housed at Strangers' Hall, where they were in the courtyard from 1932 to 1955. After being in storage for many years they have recently been put on display at the Bridewell Museum in Norwich.

EDWARD'S LEGACY

It is beyond doubt that the Blakely firm made shawls of the highest quality. In Agnes Strickland's book *Lives of the Queens of England*, published in 1852, in which she mentioned Queen Philippa's house in Norwich, she stated that she obtained her information about the house from Mr [Edward] Blakeley and described him as:

> a gentleman who contributes in no slight degree to the prosperity of the metropolis of our eastern counties, and whose school of design has carried the fine arts in wool and silk to a degree of perfection which no foreign loom can surpass.

She also remarked that:

> Queen Philippa would be astonished if it were possible for her to see the exquisite texture, colours, and patterns of some of the Norwich shawls and dresses that have been recently produced at Blakeley's manufactories.[69]

The Art Journal illustrated another of the Blakely shawls, accompanied by this tribute to their products:

> Mr. BLAKELY, of Norwich, contributes some splendid SHAWLS, woven expressly for the Exhibition. Our space does not permit us to enlarge upon the beauty

and merits of those we have here engraved; it must suffice to say they are of the very best order of design, material, and workmanship.[70]

It is a tragedy that the business failed so soon after its success at the Great Exhibition. Although Edward Blakely was not the only Norwich textile retailer to suffer the indignity of bankruptcy, he was certainly one of the more prominent traders to fail. During the next decade the fashion for wearing shawls ceased, although there was still a market for other textile merchandise until late in the century and several manufacturers were able to stay in business.

But it is good to be able to record that some of Edward's work is still in existence in Norwich. The Costume and Textile Study Centre in Norwich, now housed in the Shirehall, has several examples of shawls which were made by the Blakelys and these may be seen by prior arrangement. Three books, written by two of the foremost authorities on Norwich shawls, include illustrations of shawls attributed to the Blakely firm: these are *The Norwich Shawl*, by Pamela Clabburn; *Shawls*, by the same author; and *The Story of the Norwich Shawl*, by Helen Hoyte.[71] Plate 10 shows a corner of a shawl which Edward displayed on his stand at the Great Exhibition; it is made of black silk and worsted with gold-covered yarn woven into the motifs. It provides a fitting conclusion to this account of the work of one of the best shawl merchants of Norwich.

Corner of an Edward Blakely shawl in a private collection
Photograph © David Blakely
Plate 10

CHAPTER FIVE NOTES

1. Francis Blomefield, *An Essay towards a Topographical History of the County of Norfolk* (London, 1806), vol. III, pp. 86, 88, 612; Agnes Strickland, *Lives of the Queens of England* (London, 1852), pp. 551–2.
2. Edward T. Blakely, *History of the Manufactures of Norwich* (Norwich, n.d. [July 1850]), p. 20; previously published anonymously in *The Journal of Design and Manufactures* (London, 1850), vol. III, no. 13 March, pp. 9–11, no. 14 April, pp. 47–9, no. 16 June, pp. 106–8.
3. *Norfolk Chronicle*, 26 February and 8 April 1820. Much of the information about Edward Blakely's business is found in reports and advertisements in East Anglian and other newspapers, including the *Norfolk Chronicle*, the *Bury and Norwich Post*, the *Norfolk News*, the *Ipswich Journal*, *The Times* and the *Morning Chronicle*. References are given only in particularly significant cases and when direct quotations are made.
4. W. Chase & Co., *The Norwich Directory* (Norwich, 1783), p. 41.
5. 'Inscriptions on the memorial tablets in St. Mary's', a typewritten list compiled by C.B. Jewson, Norwich Millennium Library, L 286. St Mary's was destroyed by enemy action in 1942.
6. North Walsham Marriage Register, 1791, p. 129, no. 422, NRO, PD 711/10.
7. Thomas Peck, *The Norwich Directory* (Norwich, 1802), p. 36.
8. St Peter Mancroft marriage register, 1820, p. 58, no. 174, NRO, PD 26/12.
9. Peck, *Norwich Directory*, 1802, p. 36.
10. Chase, *Norwich Directory*, 1783, p. iv.
11. Nikolaus Pevsner and Bill Wilson, *Norfolk 1: Norwich and North-East* (Yale, 2002), p. 321.

12. Blakely, *Manufactures of Norwich*, p. 23.

13. Norwich, Old Meeting (Independent): Burials, 1751–1837, TNA, RG 4/653.

14. Private Ledger of Thomas Theobald of Norwich, 1796–1837, pp. 43, 49, NRO, BR 300/1.

15. William Dalrymple was a surgeon at the Norfolk and Norwich Hospital from 1812 until his retirement in 1839. G.T. Bettany, 'Dalrymple, William (1772–1847)', rev. Michael Bevan, in *DNB* [accessed 23 December 2015].

16. Private Ledger of Thomas Theobald, p. 54. Before the document was produced at his bankruptcy hearing in 1837 he crossed out most of the words quoted, but they are still legible.

17. St Mary's Baptist Church, Norwich, Second Church Book, pp. 72–4, NRO, FC 6, MS 4283.

18. *The Patriot* (a newspaper for Congregational Dissenters), 4 February 1841.

19. *Huntingdon, Bedford & Peterborough Gazette*, 3 December 1831.

20. *Bury and Norwich Post*, 9 March 1831. The firm was also known as Messrs Shickle, Towler and Campin.

21. *Bury and Norwich Post*, 20 April 1831.

22. *Ipswich Journal* and *Suffolk Chronicle*, 5 January 1833, quoting *Norwich Mercury*; *Derby Mercury*, 23 January 1833.

23. *Ipswich Journal*, 19 August 1837, quoting *Norwich Mercury*; copied in several other papers in other parts of the country.

24. *Bury and Norwich Post*, 13 April 1842. The advertisement was repeated, with minor variations, in other papers in the following two months.

25. Nikolaus Pevsner, *The Buildings of England, North-east Norfolk and Norwich* (1st edition, Harmondsworth, 1962), p. 284.

26. *Norfolk Chronicle*, 2 June 1810; *Norfolk News*, 4 June 1853.

27. College of Arms Grants 46.326.

28. Travel diary of Edward T. Blakely, NRO, MC 2163/1, 925X6.

29. William Hardy Cozens changed his surname to Cozens-Hardy in August 1842 in accordance with the will of his maternal

uncle William Hardy of Letheringsett in Norfolk. Some later members of the family were prominent lawyers, including W.H. Cozens's second son Herbert Cozens-Hardy, who was Master of the Rolls from 1907 to 1918.

30. Fillover shawls were woven on a draw loom, which allowed more elaborate patterns to be woven than on a hand loom. The term is exclusive to the Norwich shawl industry.

31. Helen Caroline Colman, *Jeremiah James Colman, A Memoir* (London, 1905), p. 69.

32. *Norfolk Chronicle*, 17 March 1849.

33. *Norfolk Chronicle*, 27 October 1849.

34. Sir John Boileau's letter was dated 24 March 1849, NRO, BL/F 1/36.

35. Report, Prov. Sch. of Design, p. 27; P.P. 1850 xlii 730.

36. Ibid., p. 29.

37. Marjorie Allthorpe-Guyton with John Stevens, *A happy eye: a school of art in Norwich 1845–1982* (Norwich, 1982), p. 59.

38. *Norfolk News*, 7 May 1853.

39. Plate 8 shows Edward's advertisement for Norwich Shawls in Charles Dickens, *David Copperfield*, no. XIV (London, June 1850). It is reproduced by permission from the copy held at the British Library.

40. *Norfolk Chronicle*, 8 November 1851.

41. *Norfolk Chronicle*, 5 July 1851.

42. Sir Samuel Morton Peto was a prominent industrialist whose companies were involved in the construction of railways and public buildings. From 1844 he was a member of the Baptist church and he donated large sums to charitable purposes. He was one of the financial backers of the Great Exhibition. M.H. Port, 'Peto, Sir (Samuel) Morton, first baronet (1809–1889)', in *DNB* [accessed 23 December 2015]; C.R. Fay, *Palace of Industry, 1851* (Cambridge, 1951), pp. 7, 40.

43. *Illustrated London News*, 10 May 1851.

44. *The Times*, 15 June 1849.

45. Quoted in Fay, *Palace of Industry*, p. 59; Queen Victoria's Journal

is at <http://www.queenvictoriasjournals.org/>: the relevant page is that for 14 June 1851 [accessed 23 December 2015].

46. *Norfolk Chronicle*, 21 June 1851, quoting the *Morning Post*.
47. *The Art Journal Illustrated Catalogue* (London, 1851), p. 313.
48. *Norfolk Chronicle*, 2 August 1851.
49. Plate 9 is reproduced by permission from The British Newspaper Archive at <www.britishnewspaperarchive.co.uk>.
50. *The Times*, 16 October 1851; a longer description is in *Exhibition of the Works of Industry of All Nations 1851, Reports by the Juries* (London, 1852), vol. II, p. 831.
51. *London and Paris Ladies' Magazine of Fashion*, February 1852, p. 8.
52. *Norfolk News* and *Norfolk Chronicle*, 22 May 1852.
53. *Norfolk News*, 12 March 1853.
54. *London Gazette* 21431, 15 April 1853, p. 1119.
55. *London Gazette* 21438, 10 May 1853, p. 1351.
56. *The Bankruptcy and Insolvency Reports*, vol. I, June 1853, pp. 65–8; January and February 1854, pp. 220–30. Other details of the extremely complicated court cases are to be found in newspaper reports in the summer of 1853.
57. *Norfolk News*, 2 July 1853.
58. The sale of Edward's shop in London Street was advertised in *Norfolk News*, 7 May 1853. The sale of the contents of his business premises and of his house was announced in *Norfolk News*, 14 May 1853. The notice of the sale of his house was in *Norfolk News*, 4 June 1853. The details of the sale of Edward T's manufacturing equipment were in *Norfolk News*, 11 June 1853.
59. *London Gazette* 21453, 1 July 1853, p. 1867.
60. *London Gazette* 21475, 13 September 1853, pp. 2525–6; 21476, 16 September 1853, p. 2562; V. Markham Lester, *Victorian Insolvency* (Oxford, 1995), p. 67.
61. Details from a sale advertisement in *Norfolk News*, 26 November 1859. In the spring of 1860 a boot and shoe manufacturer, P. Haldinstein, moved in. He extended the premises on the west side and they later became known as Bally's Shoe Factory. Both

parts of the building remain to this day.

62. "It was often necessary to continue the operation of the bankrupt's business until it could be profitably sold or otherwise liquidated." Lester, *Victorian Insolvency*, p. 4.

63. *London Gazette* 22005, 26 May 1857, p. 1864.

64. *London Gazette* 22014, 23 June 1857, p. 2181; Lester, *Victorian Insolvency*, pp. 17, 45. Edward's entire stock was bought by Jeffery, Morrish & Co., a Liverpool firm of silk mercers, for almost £5,000. *Liverpool Mercury*, 17 July 1857.

65. The meeting was on 30 March 1848. *Norfolk Chronicle*, 1 April 1848; *Norwich Mercury*, 8 April 1848.

66. William C. Ewing, 'Norwich Merchant Marks', in *Norfolk Archaeology,* vol. III, 1852, pp. 196–7.

67. T.J. Pettigrew, 'On the Antiquities of Norfolk', in *The Journal of the British Archaeological Association*, March 1858, p. 17.

68. John Adey Repton, 'On the Posts anciently placed on each side of the Gates of Chief Magistrates of Cities in England', in *Archaeologia or Miscellaneous Tracts relating to Antiquity*, Society of Antiquaries of London, vol. XIX, 1821, pp. 383–5.

69. Strickland, *Lives of the Queens of England*, p. 552. The author quoted Mr Blakeley, who wrote to her to say that a relative of Mrs Blakeley was then living in a later house on the site of Queen Philippa's house in The Close; this was their daughter Ellen Mary, who ran a ladies' boarding school there with her sister Eliza.

70. *The Art Journal Illustrated Catalogue*, p. 103.

71. Pamela Clabburn, *The Norwich Shawl* (London, 1995), catalogue numbers 92 and 122; Pamela Clabburn, *Shawls* (Princes Risborough, 2002), pp. 27, 29, 39; Helen Hoyte, *The Story of the Norwich Shawl* (Norwich, 2010), p. 66.

6

LATER TIMES

The preceding chapters have looked in detail at the lives of three of the four sons of John and Elizabeth Blakely and some of the family's ancestors, but the book would be incomplete without reference being made to their descendants. Of their six children only John and Edward have descendants who are still living today. The fourth son, Thomas Martin the haberdasher, married Charlotte Bond: they had a daughter who did not marry and a son who went to India. The last of their son's family died in 1965. Both of John and Elizabeth's daughters, Mary Elizabeth and Jane, died unmarried, as did Captain William Rix Blakely.

The family and some of the descendants of John Rix Blakely and his wife Naomi have been mentioned in chapter 3. In fact, it was only through their son William that they had grandchildren who lived into the twentieth century. Their eldest son John moved to Kent, where he was a grocer. He married in 1848 and in the following year was living just south of the River Thames in London, where his daughter was born. But both John and the baby were among 14,000 people who died in the major cholera epidemic which ravaged that part of London in the summer of 1849.

In April of the previous year William had booked a passage on the *Mediator*, on which he sailed to New York.[1] It can be assumed that he had intended to settle in North America, but by the time of the English census of 1851 he was living in

Norwich, working as a superintendent in a factory. His speedy return was, almost certainly, at the request of his mother, who must have written to ask him to come home, for he was her only surviving son. Her four daughters were then aged between fourteen and twenty-eight; two of them married later but had no children. If William had stayed in America the story of the family would have taken a rather different course.

Edward Theobald Blakely was very involved with his father's business, as already recounted. After his bankruptcy he moved to London, where he became a civil servant at the Board of Trade; he later married and had four children. While the family business was still flourishing Edward T wrote a pamphlet about the manufactures of Norwich, from which two extracts were quoted in chapter 5. To judge by reviews in the contemporary press, it was well received as a concise account of a trade which made a major contribution to the economy of Norwich over many centuries. When he had been working at the Board of Trade for a number of years, Edward T used some of his expertise to produce a technical dictionary, particularly for the use of those studying commercial subjects.[2] This was also regarded as a useful production, and a second edition was published after he had died.

In 1856 Edward's daughter Ellen Mary married John Culley, who was a descendant of Richard Culley, the first minister of Worstead Baptist Church. Her husband's grandfather was a leading Norfolk farmer who lived at Costessey, near Norwich; he had been responsible for building the Corn Exchange in Norwich in 1828 and his portrait used to hang there. Edward's daughter Eliza, who was friendly with the Colman family, lived in Norwich and elsewhere, but she never married.

With the advent of the twentieth century it became less common for families to remain in one place for several generations, and members of the Blakely family moved to different areas of England, with a few going abroad to

Canada and Australia. But the marks of the family's origin in a small Suffolk village near the border with Norfolk remain. Goswold Hall has been altered and extended several times over the centuries, both during and after the occupation of the Greys, the Rixes and the Blakelys, and the farm is no longer worked by the Hall's owners. Thrandeston church remains in use: in its chancel hang two hatchments which Edward, Thomas Martin and Mary Elizabeth Blakely donated in memory of their parents and brother William Rix. One hatchment impales the Blakely arms with those of Martin and the other has the cadency mark for a third son, the mullet or five-pointed star, at the centre. In the churchyard are the three family table tombs which the Blakely brothers and their sister had rebuilt; the inscriptions have become worn over the years, but they have been recorded for the use of future generations. Worstead Baptist Church in the north of Norfolk is still used for services, although with a rather smaller congregation than in the early nineteenth century. Several members of the Revd John Rix Blakely's family are buried in the graveyard.

It is to be hoped that the stories of the three brothers and their grandfather have been of interest to readers living in a very different age from the eighteenth and nineteenth centuries. Trade with China is still a major factor in the economy of the West, but the methods of transportation would be unrecognisable to Captain Blakely. Ladies' fashions change with every generation, but some of the Norwich weavers' intricate work may still be seen. Baptist churches still flourish in many places, albeit with services which are rather shorter than in John Blakely's time. And William Blakely the coachmaster would be amazed at the speed at which people can now travel from Ipswich to London. In another 200 years trade and travel may be very different again.

CHAPTER SIX NOTES

1. New York Passenger Lists, 1820-1891 at <https://familysearch.org/ ark:/61903/1:1:27GT-QKB> from National Archives and Records Administration, Washington, D.C., microfilm M237 [accessed 6 June 2014].
2. Edward T. Blakely, *A Handy Dictionary of Commercial Information* (London, 1878; reissued 1879). Second edition: *A Popular Technical Dictionary of Commercial and General Information* (London, 1885).